No Thanks:
7 Ways to Say
I'll Just Include
Myself

A Guide to Rockstar Leadership for Women of Color In the Workplace

L. MICHELLE SMITH

ISBN: 978-1-7354706-0-3

Cover design by: no silos communications llc.
Printed in the United States of America
For bulk orders for organizations, call
800.493.7950 x 06.

Visit lmichellesmith.com for more.

DEDICATION

Dedicated to my darling daughter Joni.
You can do anything! Remember that.
Mommy

CONTENTS

FOREWORD

This is for Black women and other women of color — "stuck in the middle" in the corporate workplace and fantasizing about being a boss, a leader, owning her own destiny or business. The leadership pipeline has ruptured exactly where she sits. Sponsorship seems unattainable. She is overqualified for her current role and previous ones too. She sees others easing up through the ranks with little effort. She's asking: "What do they know that I don't?" She feels sidelined. She's been in her current role and others comparable to it for years and just doesn't know how to move up. She has an urge in her gut that there has to be something more to this thing called success. She's toying with the idea of entrepreneurship because she's seen it happen for her sisterfriends, but may think she isn't cut out for it.

Covid-19, civil unrest and a huge global movement have broken out and she's "feeling some kind of way" because her employer has asked her to speak at a town hall about race. She's fed up, but doesn't know how to express it in a constructive way, ask for what she believes she's entitled to and keep her job all at once because she knows layoffs are coming and doesn't want to be on that list. She is an overworked high achiever, an innovator and a high performer who finds herself debating each year over an

1

incremental increase. Promotions continue to pass her by. She may not even think executive coaches exist and if she does, they aren't for her because, well, how do you get one anyway? She isn't even privy to all the executive perks that the one or two black senior leaders have at their fingertips that can give her a shot at generational wealth. She needs guidance, and she needs someone to provide clarity around her goals. She wants to move forward faster because her current situation isn't cutting it. She is my client... but before she met me. So here we were, somewhat happy that someone had finally seen us. Then the 2017 McKinsey/Leanin.org Women in the Workplace Study and a study by Catalyst Research finally revealed what we were already feeling and knew to be true—women of color, especially Black women, were experiencing bias, discrimination and microaggressions in the workplace more than anyone. Later in 2019, we felt somewhat heard, as authors began to give voice to our struggles in books like Minda Harts' *The Memo*, and corporations began to give rise to employee resource groups and networks just for women of color to talk about these issues. But something in the Catalyst study confirmed what we suspected. The U.S. Census revealed that women of color, led again by Black women, were starting businesses at a faster clip than any other group. Catalyst data revealed the reason: Black women were opting out of the B.S. in corporate. They were tired. Despite their credentials, Black women still experienced stalled careers, rarely able to climb to C-level leadership positions. And they were qualified. Data from that same Census revealed that Black women hold more advanced degrees than any other group; and yet, succession planning remained a mystery to many of them. While some black women take the leap into entrepreneurship, many who remain in corporate do not think that is an option for them. However, entrepreneurship is more than a state of being or a title. It is a mindset, and I contend that an entrepreneurial mindset can begin to dismantle invisible chains that hold Black women hostage in low and mid-level roles. We seem tethered to the White and male-centric power center that is at the core of the business world today—especially in the corporate workplace. The year is 2020, and all of its crises demand that we have an entrepreneurial mindset. It is at the core of transformational leadership, and according to experts, these companies want just that: someone who can manage through and ignite change.

Enter the fractured, digital and cultural economy
I shared on "The Culture Soup Podcast®" that I believed 2020 ushered in the "three beasts of the apocalypse." The three beasts are a catastrophic failure in leadership at the highest levels of our country, the onset and devastation of the thus-far incurable Coronavirus (aka COVID-19) and the world's collective rebuke to anti-Blackness, White supremacy and racism as a whole. The murder of George Floyd in the streets in Minneapolis spurred the last beast. It happened while we all watched video on the news captured by smart devices. It tipped off what many are calling the largest civil rights movement in the history of the world.

You see, before 2020, we lived in an era that was mostly called "the digital economy," where companies expected to retain employees no longer than 3-5 years. It was a highly competitive environment where technologies like artificial intelligence were beginning to replace jobs that didn't require critical thinking skills or creativity. It also meant that if you weren't familiar with some technology basics, like social media, you'd be left behind, or worse, unsearchable. Yet, the era was promising, thanks to a pretty great economy.

That changed, and quite suddenly, thanks to the triangulated, smoldering crises of 2020. In addition to the competitive landscape and tech-driven environment, we are watching a nosedive in unemployment. People who thought they were otherwise secure were being laid off or furloughed with little to any notice. Hundreds of retail and restaurant locations closed at once. In some states, retail shut down a second time because of a second viral resurgence. The travel industry also took a massive blow.

Eventually these crises will end, but at the time of publication it is unclear when. Add to it the death toll in the U.S. alone, and you see health experts predicting more than 200,000 deaths by September of 2020 if people don't wear masks, social distance, wash their hands and mostly stay home. Reports say that at least ¼ of those deaths are Black Americans. If you are Black, things look bleak. Finally, with the murders of George Floyd, Amaud Aubery, Breonna Taylor and so many others, you might have concerns for your overall safety. You may believe that if Coronavirus doesn't kill you, you may become a trending hashtag. At the very least, you might believe your job is at stake, thanks to a spiraling economy.

What's a sister to do? Is there a way to taste freedom? Even in what seems like a grim situation, there is perhaps a fresh new opportunity to move with boldness and walk in your power at work. In many respects, this unprecedented time of upheaval is the perfect opportunity, as companies attempt to sort out how they will stand on the right side of history and manage through the change brought on by this triangulated crises.

This book demonstrates exactly how to take advantage of this moment in time, based on my more than 25 years of experience as a serial entrepreneur, a corporate leader and one who has also supported the C-Suite and built businesses during two separate recessions--once with only two paychecks in the bank. This book will also share anecdotes from my Black women sponsors, mentors and peers who have overcome with an entrepreneurial mindset and made it to the senior executive levels in corporate. This mindset works extremely well for women who want to remain in the corporate workplace. It isn't simply for entrepreneurs, although they can benefit from what's to come.

My approach combines an uncompromising dedication to excellence, a willingness to bet on your own brand above all others, a firm knowledge of your value and believing in it, authentic leadership, courage to confront bias in the workplace and the confidence to know your entitlement to every good thing. While every company is grappling over how to make black lives matter within their towers, now is the time for women of color, especially Black women, to make the ask, go for the promotion or next level position, negotiate that raise, assert yourselves and run to the risk. We don't know when we will ever see a perfect storm like this again. It's time we saw the message in the mess, the opportunity in the crisis.

***

INTRODUCTION

I'm different. I've never been like any of my friends or colleagues. My mindset is different. I approach things differently, whether it is my culture, my entrepreneurial spirit, the way I approach things as a woman or my drive. I bring a special flavor to a room, to an organization, to the world. You do too.

This book is my opportunity to share with you what I've learned over the past 25 years as a TV news writer/producer, an officer at some of the largest global agencies, the owner of my own agency and private practice and as a leader at a Fortune 10 company. It's about the concept of rockstar leadership. Core to it is feeling a sense of belonging, or knowing that you may not belong and being ok with it. Fancy corporations call it inclusion, and it seems to be quite trendy. I have said that inclusion is when people with power enable the powerless with power. Over the years, however, I've learned from experience and from some of the greatest leaders, that there is another aspect to inclusion. It is very possible to empower yourself. It does take great mentorship and sponsorship, but once someone else has poured into you the right "stuff," you have cultivated the skills and you have champions willing to knock down doors for you, you can indeed create your own sense of belonging, no matter what is going on around you.

The next pages in this book unravel that for you, and they surround the idea of knowing your story and your value and putting it to work. It unravels aspects of the importance of personal branding and how it is a critical tool on the road to rockstar leadership. We also take a look at how important it is to work your 'magic' outside of the company to impact what happens inside of it. We'll explore the paradox of authenticity in a Black woman's world and how confronting microaggressions may go hand in hand. Most importantly, we delve into the idea of how, we, as women of color, those so-called "double outsiders," can lean into positive aspects of privilege and come out on top. We'll even "flip" White privilege along the way. However, it all begins with a mindset that embraces and spurs change. Some have called it running to the risk, and it's entrepreneurial in nature. The word risk scares most of us, and as a result, we are stagnant and not moving forward.

As any good coach will tell you, if you're stuck, you need to ask yourself a couple powerful questions, then reach for an affirmation or two. This book has seven, the most perfect number. Sis, I'm sending all the positive vibes your way because you're going to need them. You will also need a tribe that will pour into you, center you and provide the push you need to get to executive leadership.

There are indeed biases in the workplace, but they are

not insurmountable. I primarily view things through the lens of a Black woman, because I am one; however, you will find that there are nuggets throughout for anyone who feels left out for any reason.

Now, are you ready to do the work and speak into existence the boss status you're entitled to? What will you say to yourself to affirm that it is just fine to include yourself even when others doubt you or move in bias against you? I have several suggestions that have worked for me in the pages that follow. At the end, you'll find a coaching guide where you can take notes. I'm excited for you!

***

Guiding Principle:
1 ENGAGING AN ENTREPRENEURIAL MINDSET

F irst, allow yourself to dream again. Go back to when you were younger and less jaded by the things of the world. What did you say you wanted to be or do? Allow that to inspire you again.

I will never forget sitting in the swank office of a senior leader at my previous company. Only a month before, I'd received a notice that others may have dreaded. They called it a surplus notice. It's a very humane approach to layoffs. Once you are notified that your position has been eliminated, you have 60 days to find another position in the company, or move on with a nice lump sum depending on your tenure and rank. January 28, 2019, was the date on the heading of that email, which ultimately brought me to his office. He wanted to discuss opportunities at the company--opportunities for me to stay. Apparently, quite a few other officers held this same interest in my staying. They'd been talking. Some even called me after hours. I'd racked up quite an award-winning record at the company and had formed some incredible relationships in the C-Suite along the way. To be honest, I wasn't torn between staying or leaving; however, I wanted to see what opportunities might be unearthed at this company that I loved. On the other hand, I knew what I had to do. I had opportunities coming from other companies, extremely good ones. Then there was this little seedling of a business that I'd started on the side. Content creation was at its core: a podcast, which started as a way to expand my reach as an author, and a mentoring platform.

As I sat there drinking Topo Chicos with this, possibly one of my most admired leaders of all times, it hit me. I had made a list when I was entering graduate school. The list wasn't a bucket list. It was a list of accomplishments I wanted to achieve once I had more experience, credentials, contacts and clout. I turned to this leader and told him that I'd just realized that I only had two more items on the list to strike. I could remember the list clearly:

1. Write books
2. Speak, travel and get paid for it
3. Lecture at a university
4. Consult
5. Appear frequently on TV as a subject matter expert on culture
6. Have a family

I had already visited and pitched a book idea to one of the Big 5 publishers twice, with a third meeting pending. In 2016, the non-stop speaking tour began by happenstance, filling in for this very leader. Only a year later, my alma mater offered me my first honorarium for a keynote. I'd already been guest lecturing there and at another university in the area, so seeking an adjunct position seemed like a piece of cake. I already had the beginnings of a consulting business on the side, along with my little, vivacious, 2nd grade pumpkin. It felt like the right time to take a shot and put a bow on my dreams.

Fortunately, my mentor/sponsor, this officer was extremely open-minded about what I had to say. He was one of the few that recognized my skills as a businesswoman and what that entrepreneurial spirit brought to the company. He knew the strength of my big picture vision and my ability to scale most anything if given the reins and budget. A little bit of encouragement, and I could make it happen better than imagined. I always had returned more than he had invested.

I knew what I had done at the company to be about entrepreneurship, but business books called this transformational leadership. It is the thing that separates managers from leaders because it involves change. Transformational leaders are people who can instigate change or lead through it. They are builders and fixers. They don't sit still for very long. They read tealeaves and have a penchant for what's next.

I would ultimately make the decision to leave the big company, but without the promise of anything solid as my next step. Who does that? Someone with opportunities does that. I had the ability to weigh them out. Surely enough, sometime within two months, I had my answer, despite offers to build from scratch and run the corporate communications department of an international restaurant chain.

I would ultimately bet on me. I call myself "untethered." All throughout my career, whether on someone else's payroll or on my own, I've had choices. I didn't realize it until I made a decision to walk away from an officer role at a global agency simply to "try out" consulting. That resulted in my running a successful boutique agency for nearly a decade. So giving myself permission to be a little risky paid dividends, and while seamlessly moving into and out of corporate, my mindset has been different ever since.

It's time to untether with an *entrepreneurial mindset*. I believe it is time women of color, especially Black women, untethered themselves. Some call the feelings of comfort that tie us to one company "golden handcuffs." It's that comfort zone of the steady paycheck that has hypnotized many of us into thinking that it is the only state of being-- that we should cling to that steady paycheck and the promise of incremental bonuses and great benefits from one source for dear life. Our parents called it stability. Shifting your mindset to an entrepreneurial one, approaching your "self" as a business entity all its own, is the way to get unbound But it takes some powerful self- talk.

My perspective on an entrepreneurial mindset has three aspects to it: *Intraprenuership* was a term introduced years ago by Xerox. These are individuals who build business ecosystems within existing ones. *Entrepreneurship* is the term that most people associate with going at business alone where you put people and processes in place in order to grow thriving business ecosystems. The final term is my own. I call it *"extrapreneurship."* It is my retort to the ever-popular term "side hustle." For those of us who are educated, credentialed and experienced, this term elevates the idea of running a business while working for another entity full time. After all, a hustle truly is chasing the next "get" without a true plan in place; and it is living from this thing to that, with the only real objective being to get money. Knowing how to and actually being all three of these concepts allows you to say, "No thanks, I'll simply include myself," and it is the story of my life.

This entrepreneurial mindset also allows you to put your current 9-5 in perspective. Should you really be living to work for a company? I understand that has been the unspoken culture in Corporate America, but it's unhealthy, unrealistic and limiting. Only the company wins at that game. Allowing what you do from 9 to 5 to fuel your passions and pursuits should be the goal. That is a win-win. Leveraging the learnings and experiences from that position to provide you with vision for your next—that's optimal. What I describe is based on the NSC Coaching Priorities Hierarchy for Leadership™. It places self ahead of your home and career. It is based on basic tenets in applied positive psychology that happy people are successful people, not the other way around. Society teaches us to chase success first, and we will find happiness. Science reveals just the reverse.

For those sisters of faith, never fear. Self-care isn't selfish. In fact, for those of you who are Bible-based, remember that after loving your God before anyone, the Scripture says to love your neighbor as yourself. The underlying premise is that you have to love yourself as a baseline before you are even able to fathom what it means to love someone else. Prioritizing self is not selfish. Everyone benefits. Imagine if we prioritized ourselves how much happier we'd be and equipped to love and nurture our family and relationships. Imagine how we'd be able to absolutely kill it at work. We will begin this mindset shift with some basic ideals that will provide you with an "inside out, outside in" mentality, and carry you through this journey of affirmations and coaching exercises. Remember, you must lean out to win at leaning in where you work.

1. **Prioritize learning how to build business inside a company that can fund your pursuits with that steady paycheck**. Then, profit from your achievements. You will profit from the experience while working for someone else.

2. **Begin to diversify your income sources outside of your job and build business ventures.** Some of these simply require some reading and searching on Google. Getting into investments like short-term real estate is a great example. Starting a business isn't the only way.

3. **Build your personal brand intentionally, internally and externally.** This will build your options and attract opportunities inside and outside of your current position.

4. **LEAP *when* you want, *where* you want and *even* if you are pushed.** But most importantly, leap *how* you want to reach that next big role or venture.

Coaching questions: What would you like to achieve as you go on this journey to shift your mindset to an entrepreneurial one? How might you engage one, two or all three of the aspects of this mindset to get to your goal?

✳✳✳

Now, repeat these seven things to yourself each day. Place them on stickies everywhere you can. Write them in large print on your vision boards. It's time you became the rockstar leader you've always wanted to be. Get your journal and pen handy. Let's go!

✳✳✳

Affirmation 1:

2 "I KNOW WHO I AM, AND I FIND VALUE IN MY STORY."

The year was 2016. One of the top executives at my company took an interest in me and became my mentor. I literally didn't think I had done anything to spur this, but apparently I had. He walked by my workspace one day and told me to get on his calendar, so I did. I thought I had a new business unit to support. So, I showed at the appointed time with my pen and paper and asked him how could I support. And he said pretty pointedly, "No, how can I help you?"

I was stunned. Here I was, at nearly the top floor of this skyscraper, sitting across from one of the most powerful men at this company. He happened to be Black, and he actually asked me what he could do to help a level two manager. Well, I'll be, I thought to myself. I had happened upon a pocket of Black privilege at this extremely White, yet by any standards diverse, company. I knew exactly what I had to do. Members of my tribe, my personal board of directors, had prepared me for it. They told me always to have "an ask" when I finally get the attention and time of someone of rank. And I had one.

"Is it possible that I could join one of your mentor circles?" I asked. He politely declined because he said he was just disbanding one, but if I would get on his books once monthly for 30 minutes, he would carve out time for us to talk about anything I wanted.

My mind was blown, and I thanked him, probably about five times before leaving his office. Then he asked an extremely curious question:

"Please don't take offense to this when I say it, but I have to ask, what are you doing here?" There was an extremely awkward pause. Was this a trick question? So I started to chronicle how my former boss from the global agency was embedded at the company and one day the phone rang and... "

"No, that isn't what I'm asking," he said. "Why are you here? You are too good for this place." Full stop. Could this meeting get any more awkward? Then he said, "...with your talent, you could go anywhere. You are smart, and you are hip and fashionable...I just want to know what made you come to this company? It isn't ready for you. Don't get mad at me for saying this."

So, I explained that I wasn't angry. I was more confused than anything. Here I was, talking to one of the highest-ranking men of color at this gigantic company, peering over the expanse of DFW from the top of a skyscraper, in an office with floor-to-ceiling windows that turned the entire corner of the building. This man had to be one of the smartest men in the industry and others too. Fine clothes, fine credentials, probably a fine car (I hadn't seen yet)...you know, that well-heeled Black executive that this company was known to produce: sheer Black excellence manifested in the flesh. And he asked me what, exactly?

I really didn't have an answer, and he said that was OK, instructed me to book the next session the following month, and we'd go from there. I didn't know my value. That's what this man was trying to tell me. I couldn't even hear it. I didn't believe it, but something would happen between that next session and now that would change all that. That same executive offered to sign me up for Executive Leadership Council's (ELC) Strategic Pathways Leadership training program. I used to joke that this was the Illuminati of Black Corporate America because only those who knew, knew, and oh boy, were they powerful and rich.

Really, it was a joke. I actually knew exactly what the organization was and had the honor of representing one of the founding member's companies when I ran my agency in the early 2000's. It was one of my first big clients: Pro- line International. Its founder was Comer Cottrell, one of the founding members of the ELC.

I'd been to one of their galas as a guest of their vice president and general manager (VPGM), at the time, Sheryl Adkins-Green and her husband, Geoff. The ELC's membership spanned the globe. Their mission is to fill the Fortune 500 pipeline with the finest Black leaders through training, mentoring, coaching and advocacy.

I was thrilled to have this opportunity. My SVP at the time, one of the most supportive White male advocates I've had, signed off on the opportunity just shortly after promoting me to director, and soon I would find myself standing toe-to-toe with this woman who kind of scared me. But I liked it! This would be the beginning of uncovering my value, but it wouldn't happen without an intense conversation about chicken fries in front of 150 Black women leaders from Fortune 500 companies from all over the nation.

Awkward. But, you'll find my life is full of awkward moments, but just on the other side...BAM...opportunity!

What chicken fries have to do with it...

So this very kind, yet sort of scary woman was Trudy Bourgeois, the CEO of the Center for Workforce Excellence. She is a consultant to some of the biggest corporations out there and a trainer at the ELC's Strategic Pathways program. This program was specifically crafted for Black women with leadership aspirations. Their companies tapped them as "high potential" or "hi-pos" for short. This meant that their companies saw their leadership abilities and wanted to further groom them to be the next generation of senior executives. Trudy challenged this group to try out impromptu business banter, an important skill she said we should cultivate if we had C-Suite aspirations. However, we were only afforded a glance at the headlines of a few of the nation's biggest newspapers— *USA Today, New York Times* and the *Wall Street Journal*. Luck of the draw, I picked up *The Journal*. Lo and behold, the headline was about Burger King's chicken fries. Chicken fries. *Really?* And just like that, I heard, "Ms. Smith! Stand up! I want you to banter with me. You just ran into me in the hall at work, and I'm the Chairman. Let's talk about the headlines." Well, alrighty! I stood up before my 149, soon-to-be ELC fellows, and we began to banter. Without a ton of detail, I mentioned the chicken fries. Bourgeois, playacting as the highest-ranking officer in my company, asked if there were any lessons in it for "our business," and I responded:

"Yes, what the fast food chain did was take two things that were well-known and loved by everyone and created something totally different and innovative." I mentioned how that was happening in the tech-telecom space and drew on a few examples of consumer passion points that could cross pollinate with our products and services and open new doors for the business.

What BK did wasn't really rocket science, and typically, disruption happens when things we already know are blended in ways they have never been before. So ultimately, a mash-up of chicken fingers and french fries put the chain back on the right track to record same-store sales.

That was one of the most intense five minutes in my most recent memory, but I did it! Later at a break, Trudy approached me and asked a bit more about who I was. Turns out the executive at my company had told her a little about me, but she said to me, "You know what? You've got it. You are going to go far. What do you want to do?" Like with the uncomfortable question that senior executive asked earlier, I was stumped again. *Why didn't I know?* I knew what I had been told, and I told her that, but I really didn't know for myself. Why were these pretty simple questions giving me so much angst? It was because I really didn't know my value, and I had never taken the time out for me to think through these important, yet basic questions. By the end of Leadership Week, I would, and Trudy would make sure of it. This training was cathartic. Trudy had us all map out our 10 most significant moments in life—good and bad, personal and professional—all on one continuum. In no time, the room was full of women in tears. What was this strange corporate version of "Fix My Life"?

I began to uncover my story and gather the gems that were hiding underneath: a high school standout, a collegiate stand out, columnist of the *TCU Daily Skiff* who often challenged the campus on race issues, an NCAA cheerleader, a VP before the age of 30, divorce, a near-death experience on an operating table, miscarriages, one incredible daughter, two-time homeownership (one home I built from the ground up), an incredible run as an award winning entrepreneur and at the time and an awesome run at a Fortune 10.

I began to see recurring themes: resilience, tenacity, courage, innovation and faith. Trudy explained that these lessons along life's journey would be the foundation for our leadership platform, which was squarely derived from our value. That was meta.

There are literally keys to your today and to your future and to your purpose, embedded in your past. It really is a matter of what you do with the information. Going through this soul-stretching process helped me to focus on my wins and my victories. I also had to focus on the challenging parts of my journey to get the lessons along the way. While it felt uncomfortable, it was a revealing process for me to begin to understand that I truly did bring value to all my endeavors.

What was even more dynamic? I understood that my value would not only translate in the boardroom, but it also showed up in me as a woman, in my relationships and as a mother. As I learn to assert my own value, I am sharing these skills with my daughter. Having her learn these lessons early is definitely one way I want to help her understand her value even now.

Trudy and I remain close. In fact, she is now one of my amazing mentor coaches as I scale my private coaching and consulting practice. That executive at the company is also only a text or a call away. I owe them a debt of gratitude for seeing me, thrusting me into potent pockets of privilege and guiding me to the knowledge of my worth. In fact, my current company's original master class and webinar platform was branded 'The 30 Minute Mentor", inspired by that executive who asked me the awkward question that day in his office.

Through my own mentoring efforts, I began to pour into other professionals what he poured into me, 30 minutes at a time. That platform eventually made way for my executive and business coaching practice and my elearning platform. My clientele have always been primarily women seeking to know their value and the doors that could open for them.

Knowing your value is core to the mindset that untethers you from all that holds you back, including the expectations of others. It is a growth mindset that says that failures are simply happenings, mere incidences in time. You learn from them. Then you move forward. A growth mindset understands that failure does not define you.

In this case, failures are the very building blocks that make you stronger and even more valuable. They point you to your purpose. With this knowledge, you can build a solid and compelling *value proposition*. Your value proposition is one sentence that tells what problem you solve.

Valuing your roots

I now develop rockstar leaders and brands that thrive at the intersection of tech, culture and business. I do it through writing, speaking, coaching and advising Fortune 100 professionals and small business owners. That is my value proposition, and I didn't just pull that out of the sky because it sounded good. It is rooted in my authentic journey. In fact, looking back, I uncovered a list that I made in graduate school of all the things I wanted to do and couldn't because I was fresh out of college with no credibility or experience. I'm doing all of those things today! Simply put, my value proposition is my story put to action for me... today.

Here's an example of how it works. This is my technology story: Long before I ever stepped a foot into corporate America, technology was a vital part of my story. Growing up in Texas with a fairly progressive father, I learned to program (or code, as they say today) BASIC on some of the very first computers that were ever introduced into the consumer marketplace. I took that knowledge to college with me. I didn't have an Internet connection in my dorm room, but I had to finish computer-programing requirements for my degree. I learned Paschal on mainframe computers. I know this is dating me, but remember technology moves fast! Coding on a mainframe sounds very *Hidden Figures*, but even in the 90s, that dreaded journey to the lab at night actually gave me some real confidence to tackle more modern coding languages for that time. From there, I taught myself HTML while I was bored on the job at the home offices of a large retailer. This was technically my first corporate job after working as a writer/producer at a local TV station. One of my first entrepreneurial ventures was creating a message board for members of my sorority and for those who were interested in becoming members. They could find each other, connect, and share information across the country and even internationally. This was in the mid-90s long before Facebook came to the masses or Instagram was even a thing. I didn't think of monetizing my idea, but looking back, it could have been my first chance to have a business outside of my day job. As I explored both corporate and entrepreneurial opportunities throughout my career, I discovered that one of my greatest values was in my knowledge of technology. An outgrowth of that was my entrepreneurial spirit.

I developed the balance of my value proposition in that ELC workshop, and it has yielded one award-winning concept that I launched at the Fortune 10 where I worked.

Later, it produced six incredible brands that form the core of my small business. It also tells the story of my life. Even the position at the big company makes plenty of sense when you look back at it through the lens of my value proposition. I literally built their diversity and inclusion corporate communications and integrated marketing practice in their global marketing organization from scratch. We won awards, and I was asked to speak on stage about it nonstop. I was an intrapreneur. That's rockstar leadership thriving at the intersection of tech, culture and business made manifest in my life.

Uncovering your story

How do you dig into understanding your value proposition? First, you need to understand the consistent parts of your life's story and pull them to the forefront. Have you always been good with numbers? Are you great with bringing people together on a team? Are you good with finding new solutions to tough problems? Give yourself the opportunity to start creating a list of your superpowers. These are your skills.

I tell my coaching clients that these are the things you can do easily, even if someone tied you up, blindfolded you and threw you into the ocean while you were sleeping. List three of these hard skills. Then list three passions. These are the topics and subject matters that you value in both your personal and professional life. Again, I tell clients that these are the things that even on your deathbed, or as my great-grandmother used to call it your "cooling board," you wake up and say, "There's one more thing I just have to do." Think of three of those passions. After you've written out your superpowers and passions, give yourself another few moments to see how you can walk out your passions with your superpowers. Once you have your value proposition in place, observe how this currently fits into who you are within your corporate environment, at home, anywhere. It's OK if your passions and superpowers are currently out of alignment with what you're doing now. This gives you a perfect opportunity to reconfigure and realign your core values with what will make you happy and fulfilled in the long term. We are no longer in a day and age when we want to or have to be in a position for 10, 20, or 30 years just to get a paycheck and some benefits.

In fact, talent acquisition professionals are looking for people who show their agility and ability to move in and out of a variety of roles that demonstrate their critical thinking and ability to adapt to or instigate change. Think of uncovering your value through your story as your chance to create the forward motion you desire in your life in the workplace and beyond. This is not only for yourself, but for your children, your community, and those who can benefit from your showing up and bringing your higher self into whatever room you are invited. While your value is solidly rooted in your story, it begins with the fact that you are fearfully and wonderfully made, a daughter of God, entitled to every good thing.

Coaching questions: What are your three superpowers? What are your three passions? Now try your hand at a value proposition. What is your "one thing"?

***

3 "I'LL BE EXCELLENT ...AND GOOD WITH THE SKIN I'M IN."

So you want to be your authentic self in your corporate job, but the data about how to do this successfully is daunting, to say the least. McKinsey & Co., along with LeanIn.Org originally released their annual Women in the Workplace study in 2017, which included stats on women of color and Black women specifically. It seemed to result in a collective rejoicing and simultaneous sigh from women of color across the country. Finally, there was data to back what many already knew: women of color—especially Black women— have more challenges in the corporate environment than most, as they attempt to climb the ladder into the C-suite. The report shares that the complexity of gender and color actually does matter when it comes to filling the pipeline to leadership; and in many cases, women and women of color—again, especially Black women—are left behind due to lack of access to senior leadership and other factors. The report shows that at some point many Black women simply opt out to start their own companies. Consider that there are currently no Black women CEOs at Fortune 500 companies. Ursula Burns, former CEO at Xerox was the most recent, but she retired in 2016. *Fortune*'s Ellen McGirt unpacked many of the reasons in a compelling article called The Black Ceiling: "Why African-American Women Aren't Making it to the Top in Corporate America." The article calls Black women "double outsiders," referencing research from Catalyst, being neither White nor men. That means Black women are different right down to their melanin and chromosomes; they are largely foreign to a corporate culture that is used to having the exact opposite of Black women in the ranks, especially in leadership. The people in the company may expect to see Black women in support roles if they are in the environment at all. If this is true, the friction is not only natural and wrong, it is nearly unavoidable.

So what do Black women actually need to do in order to bring their most authentic selves to work and succeed, knowing all this? Understanding that the deck seems to be organically stacked against who they truly are? Women's conferences typically have panels and speakers on the topic, but what does it really mean to bring your #blackgirlmagic to work and still ascend into leadership? Is it even possible?

Sis, it's time we had this conversation. Someone asked me, "What is Bozoma Saint John's 'secret sauce'?" While I have only met and spoken with her once, she demonstrates the traits of someone who understands that she is entitled to have it all the way she wants it because she knows her value. She has centered herself and is the CEO of Brand Boz. That scares many of you. I know, because I hear this from clients and from audience members when I speak across the country.

The second reason for her meteoric success: she is not afraid to get up and move. That scares the rest of you. She has been called a unicorn, but she simply knows who she is and the value she brings, and is willing to bet on Boz. You can and should bet on you, too. You'll hear this same sentiment from executive-level Black women who have pierced the Black ceiling. They agree that all the degrees may or may not get you there. The willingness to pack up all your credentials and go to the better opportunity for you definitely will. The good news is that Ursula Burns and others have done it. So I contacted more of Corporate America's power players, all of them currently or previously in the C-suite or officers in Fortune 500s.

I asked them to give their take on whether it really is possible to walk tall in "the skin you're in" at work as a Black woman and what it actually takes. Why did I turn to these ladies? Their résumés and credentials alone qualify them, but each of them has had an incredible impact on my career over the past decade; and I know from personal experience that these women are genuinely who they are at work as well as in their daily lives. They are indeed authentic.

It should also be noted that each of these game changers is a member of the Executive Leadership Council of which I am a Fellow, having served as a coach and trainer as part of their online education series. All of this happened as a result of having the awesome opportunity to complete their Strategic Pathways leadership training and attend their annual Leadership Summit.

Being Black and unbothered is a process

In the beginning, you're Black and constantly bothered. When the CEO of the Dallas Mavericks, Cynthia "Cynt" Marshall, started her first job after graduating from the University of California at Berkeley more than 36 years ago, she was met with a superior who challenged her church clothes, braids, and "red-hooker shoes" on her first day. After plenty of tears and navigating that trying time at the impressionable age of 21, she said that by the time she was promoted to the officer ranks some 20 years later, she was far more comfortable in her skin. She said mostly, it was because she had a better idea of who she was at that point, which is crucial to walking tall in your own skin. "The person who gets out of bed in the morning is the person that walks into the building. So it's the beliefs you have, the values you have, the problems you have...all of that gets out of bed with you," Marshall said.

"You don't go into a phone booth and come out with a cape on and a logo of your company, like somebody else, some superhero. That person actually walks into the building. So what you have to try to create, especially as leaders, try to create a culture—you want a culture where that person who gets up out of the bed in the morning, walks into the door and you meet them where they live." Marshall says that it needs to be an environment where it

32

is OK for people to be themselves. What she wishes she knew on her first day is what she says she knows now: that it is important to do your homework on the company culture before you enter it. She also pointed to performance as a factor. Over a period of time, she said that the company will get to know your stellar performance, and your personal nuances will matter less and less. Marshall is the first woman CEO in the National Basketball Association and is largely credited for getting the Dallas Maverick's franchise back on track after a much- publicized sexual harassment scandal.

Cheryl Grace, senior vice president of U.S. Strategic Community Alliances and Consumer Engagement at Nielsen Inc. and CEO of PowerfulPenny.com, added that one's most authentic self is the gateway to adding value. Grace said it was sometimes challenging initially to balance her outgoing and outspoken nature with the corporate environment, and she eventually learned when to tone it down and when to turn up the volume. She said there is a time and a place for everything you bring to the table, but ultimately, mimicking other people isn't an option.

"I think it means that you shouldn't have to pretend that you're someone else to be successful. I think this is relatively unique to women, particularly women of color because historically we've either tried to run the gamut of trying to dress like men and talk like men in business situations," Grace said. She also believes that it is when you are your most natural self, you will more than likely provide unique suggestions, recommendations, and solutions; but if you are trying to think like everyone else in the room, you will not stand out. Grace said that ideally, when a company has several unique ways of looking at a situation or a business issue, that company is more likely to arrive at one solution that works for the broader universe and for their broader market.

Knowing yourself, your value and being excellent
Trudy Bourgeois, the founder and CEO of the Center for Workforce Excellence is also the author of the book *EQUALITY: Courageous Conversations About Women, Men, and Race to Spark a Diversity and Inclusion Breakthrough.* She was that presenter who pulled me aside at the Executive Leadership Council's Leadership Week for high-achieving Black executives who were looking to break into the C-suite. In those sessions, she reminds professionals to know their proud history as Black people in America. They are "daughters (and sons) of God." It's a call to action to know one's self- worth and not to accept anything but the best in their careers and lives. She says that part of the issue is that most people don't know what "authenticity" or "authentic behavior" even looks like. Bourgeois says it is far more than whether you wear your hair natural or not, or even simply about what you wear.

"They say that they want to be authentic, but they haven't defined who they really are, and as a result, they have not developed the courage to maximize what they bring to the table. We have to 'get' who we are." Bourgeios believes that we have to understand what kind of value we bring, and that sweet spot is when our passions and our capabilities align with an organization's needs because when we are in a position to demonstrate our brilliance, people will accept us for who we are. Mary Kay Chief Marketing Officer Sheryl Adkins Green has had an extremely successful track record in the beauty business but says the same rules apply in any industry. It didn't take long for her to move from vice president of marketing to CMO at the company after joining in 2009. You may remember her name from earlier, former VPGM at Pro-line International and ELC member. The Harvard Business School alumna believes Black women have to be smart about the company culture where they work then deliver that magic in doses. They must choose the time and place to shine. Stellar performance, however, is key.

"Bringing your authentic self means confidently bringing all of your talent, interests, and perspective to your role versus just a portion. Some worry that their strengths and talents might intimidate or threaten their relationship with their manager and/or team members and this can be a risk," Green said. But she says playing "small" or playing not-to-lose versus playing to win is an even riskier career strategy. Green believes that if you want to be seen as the "best," you need to bring your best to your role—every day. The key is to be savvy about how and when you "show your stuff," and you need to align your efforts with the goals of the enterprise.

Coaching question: How might you shift the way you are showing up to work in order to leverage authenticity as a leader?

***

4 "I RECOGNIZE THAT THERE IS INDEED A PROBLEM, AND I WILL CONFRONT IT."

A manifestation of bias, racism and sexism that typically rears its head in the workplace is a type of bias called microaggression. It is likely one of the most common ways people are discouraged to be their most authentic selves at work and run to the risk in order to become a rockstar leader. Microaggressions can creep up on you at the most unexpected times.

It happened to me recently as my daughter and I were enjoying lunch at the local deli. I was filling her cup up at the soda fountain when a woman asked me a question that caught me off guard. I was wearing a shirt with the French words "Ça va?" printed on the front and the phrase "Tres bien merçi" written on the back. In English, this means "How's it going?" and "Very well, thanks." Be that as it may, the woman asked me, rather pointedly, "Do you know what your shirt says?" At first, I thought maybe she wasn't talking to me. So I turned toward her and found her eyes piercing at me. That's when I realized that a White woman was preparing to give me an unsolicited French lesson right in the middle of Jason's Deli. I was being charged-up by a complete stranger to see if I was worthy of the shirt on my back. It was happening again: another White woman was placing herself in charge of me. So, with all the polite firmness and with a chuckle of irony, I said, "Of course I know what my own shirt says. I'm wearing it." But she did not relent.

"Do you know French?" she persisted. Amazed that she was still speaking to me and pursuing this line of conversation, something warmed up inside me. I looked her dead in her eye and responded, "Je parle un peu de français," or to translate, "I speak a little bit of French." Now, this was not the time to rattle off my credentials: a near-decade of French lessons from high school and college or the past 5 years as a subject matter expert in diversity, inclusion, equity and culture for the largest advertiser in the world. Nor was it the time to question if she knew that there are plenty of French-speaking people who look just like me around the globe. But, I had a good mind to really disturb her lunch. Maybe it was the Diet Dr. Pepper. Perhaps it was Jesus, but I decided instead to make it a learning moment for the woman and for my young daughter.

Yes, that woman needed to see that I was indeed the educated woman that she didn't mistake me for, and my daughter needed to see how to confront bias with the class, grace, and razor sharpness for which a situation like this calls. So, after we finished our lunch, I decided to step toward the woman's table.

"Ma'am," I said directly and firmly, but in a normal tone. "I have an English lesson for you. I need you to look up the word microaggression. Look up the word today, because that will help you understand why I did not take kindly to your approach to me. Do you understand?" The woman, mouth full of sandwich said, "I'm sorry." I grabbed my daughter's hand, and we left the restaurant. *Psychology Today* defines a microaggression as:

"The everyday verbal, nonverbal, and environmental slights, snubs, or insults, whether intentional or unintentional, which communicate hostile, derogatory, or negative messages to target persons based solely upon their marginalized group membership. In many cases, these hidden messages may invalidate the group identity or experiential reality of target persons, demean them on a personal or group level, communicate they are lesser human beings, suggest they do not belong with the majority group, threaten and intimidate, or relegate them to inferior status and treatment."

These forms of bias can happen to you whether you are Black, LatinX, Asian, Native American, a woman, a young person, a senior, someone with different abilities, LGBTQ or some other category in which society places us. And, according to Columbia University professor Derald Wing Sue, these microaggressions at work can kill your confidence. But there are some actions you can take in the workplace, whereas, on the other hand, sometimes confrontation only spawns denials and downplays of the incident as trivial or even harmless.

In the book Microaggressions in Everyday Life: Race,

Gender and Sexual Orientation, Sue writes that it is important to seek allies within the workplace who can also call out the behavior because when marginalized people do so, they are frequently told they are being too sensitive. I don't know all the reasons why the woman singled me out in the deli, but I discussed it with cultural and political journalist and "Fanti" podcast host Jarrett Hill on an episode of my show, "The Culture Soup Podcast®". I provided a little more information about the woman who tried to charge me up over what amounted to conversational French on my shirt. Hill categorized this microaggression and other examples like it with more pointed words. He said that her approach to me was an act of White privilege, but also shared that you don't have to be White to engage in it. This woman in the deli was "Karen" in full bloom over lunch. Later, we'll look at how attitudes like these can be flipped in our favor as women of color.

Now that you know, what will you do? So, now you know that it's not your imagination, my Sister. Microaggressions are real. These are actions others take actively or passively against you that belittle, discredit, discount, condescend, call out or disenfranchise you whether or not the offender knows it. Sometimes it's simply someone who places themselves in charge of you for absolutely no reason at all. Even as we approach the third decade in this new century, Black women are still facing the challenges of dealing with racism and sexism in Corporate America.

It may not be as blatant as calling you the N-word

or a B--- to your face, but these challenges are very real and it's essential that as you are glowing, flexing, and leading, that you have effective strategies for knowing how to deal with these offenses in the workplace and with anyone who underestimates your skill set. If I walk into a meeting, and I'm the only one who is brave enough to ask an insightful and pointed question, I've often heard through the grapevine later, "Why is she talking?" or "Why is she asking all these questions?" or "She always has something to say." The questions clearly needed to be asked, but if they came from one of my White peers, there would be no discussion about why a pertinent issue was raised in the first place. When you begin to question yourself about your right to speak up, your right to be, or your right to assert your authority, microaggressions have begun to eat away at the fiber of your confidence and your ability. Here is the thing about microaggressions: they do not only come from White people. We are talking about deep-seated, institutionalized feelings and perceptions about Black women. This means that these actions and passive aggressions can come from other people of color, other under-represented groups, other women, and even other Black people. Microaggressions are like subtle parasites that will eat away at your ability to be an effective member of your team, an effective leader, or to build a thriving business. Unlike the days of the civil rights movement in the 60s, there aren't any water hoses or dogs threatening your safety and well-being. In case you have hit the streets in protest during today's movement, perhaps you were faced with teargas and rubber bullets. But if in the workplace you have enough subtle microaggressions coming up and filtering through your mind on a monthly, weekly, or even daily basis, eventually the small infractions will begin to eat away at your confidence and your ability to operate in excellence.

I was fortunate to have an experience in one of my companies where the leadership team assembled a group of women of color to begin discussing what was happening to us in that corporate environment. As we began talking, we quickly understood that these small infractions were happening to all of us. What was even more eye opening was to see that this was also happening to Asian and Latinas within the company. Another caveat-

-you shouldn't always assume that White men are the adversaries. I can safely say that White men have outnumbered the Black women sponsors and advocates I've had throughout my career. That is simply because there are more White men in senior leadership in the workplace. Some White men understand and recognize a microaggression far sooner than you will. In my experience, some of these men have called out these situations before I have.

However, there is no power in being quiet or docile as you're having meetings with your colleagues. As one of my mentor coaches, LaFern Batie of The Batie Group said to me, "Sometimes we have to be willing to slam the door so that it shakes the pictures on the wall and speak in words and a tone that they can relate to." Particularly as Black women, we have to be prepared to speak up for ourselves, actively set boundaries and be on our toes to counteract bias. We can't allow someone to "mansplain" or "Whitesplain" us so that someone else receives credit for our ideas. Being known, seen, and valued in the room as a contributor to any discussion is extremely important for you. You have to realize and understand that you are just as or even more powerful, capable and agile as any of your counterparts.

Fear of what they may say about you is real for so many. Fear that they will call you angry, hard to work with, opinionated...any of the tropes assigned to Black women. If you know that is a possibility, think of the case scenario, understand who might say it. Are they the leaders or influencers in your company and industry who could impact your career? If so, is this really the environment where you can thrive?

Bias is just a no. No is a game of numbers.

If Michael Jordan had quit after he was cut from the basketball team in high school, we wouldn't know him as the legend he is today. Even standouts like Jordan have heard the word *no*. If Jackie Robinson had quit after facing racism on and off the baseball diamond, how long would we have waited to see baseball integrated? The fact is that bias is just another form of rejection, and we, as humans, have an interesting relationship with the word *no*. We struggle with when to use it for ourselves to set boundaries, especially as women. We hate to see the word coming when it is headed our way; however, we must learn to expect it. When you think about it, *no* is a game of numbers. In life, in sales, in relationships, the *nos* will always outnumber the *yesses*, and while this isn't my invitation to be pessimistic, it truly is an opportunity to be optimistically realistic.

We must learn to calculate the times we hear *no*, and look expectantly for the *yes* that will follow. Event planners will tell you 20% of a guest list might actually show up to your party. Marketers will say to expect an 18% average open rate on your email campaign. Paid search experts will tell you to expect a conversion rate somewhere between 10-15%. You get the drift. There will always be more *no*s than *yesses*, so if you consider the odds, *no*s, rejections, bias even, are less scary.

We should embrace *no*s because rejection breeds tenacity and resilience, that is if you keep going. Rockstar leaders are tenacious and resilient. *No* for these leaders is the pathway to *yes*. In fact, *no* makes the way to *yes* more defined, and informs us to get to yes faster and make that yes even more delicious.

We must not take *no* personally. Now, this is a hard one, especially where bias is involved, because many times it can be. Your feelings are up to you, however. When faced with racism or sexism, I've chosen to believe that the other party wouldn't simply express bias to me, they'd more than likely do it to a whole group of us. I just happen to be in their path in this particular situation. Do you choose to see *no*, rejection or bias as failure? How will you use the lesson to get to your *yes*?

Rockstar leaders eat *no* for breakfast. So, have some coffee with your *no* next time. Expect a few more, but many *no*s make the *yesses* far sweeter.

Coaching question: The next time you are faced with a microaggression, bias or rejection, how will you respond?

***

Affirmation 4:

5 "I WILL BE MY BEST ADVOCATE."

Are you strong enough to know when it's time to bow out of a bad situation and actually do it? Do you know when it's time to leave even when the situation is good, yet safe? Remember that the demand for your excellent talent is a valuable resource.

You can always change positions or pursue another entrepreneurial path. As one of my mentor coaches told me, you should always keep a stash of funds so that when it's time for you to leave, you have enough savings in the bank that'll hold you over until you find the next perfect opportunity. That's whether you've secured another already or not. We are no longer in the day and age when you just have to stick it out and suck it up. You have options to preserve your sanity and create the next position or a new venture that will be perfect for you. Whenever you find yourself overwhelmed and stressed, this is a signal that this position isn't the right fit for you. Particularly as an entrepreneur, if you are running up against the same challenges with the same investors or contractors, know that you have the freedom to explore other opportunities. Even if you are in a position where you feel like you have to hold onto a job to take care of your family and maintain your financial stability, go back to your value proposition, and understand that you can get a new position. You don't have to hold onto the mindset that says that you have to stay in one job for the rest of your life. Use your personal board and brand to see that there are new opportunities everywhere and that you don't have to chase them. They will chase you.

As you are thinking about transitioning into a new position or going for that promotion, make sure that you are accessing and activating your tribe as you are making your next move. Tap into your mentors and discover what skills you need to build before you move forward to a new position. Please don't shy away from your sponsors. They really are there to help you get where you want to go. They can see around corners that you can't, and they will be in rooms where you won't. Remember the high- ranking gentleman at the big company where I worked? He also challenged me to explore my market value, and while this was by no means his invitation for me to leave the company, it was definitely his way of suggesting I look outside in order to look inside of me and know my worth. As a result, I could walk taller and take greater risks where I was planted. You really do have to lean out to lean in to your best work, especially when you decide to stay at that company and climb. This will build your confidence. You will begin to know and understand that no one company can or should own you.

This new mindset will allow you to make better decisions. You can also remain alert and open to the opportunities that you attract. Remember that nothing has to be wrong at work for you to make a move. Grabbing change by the horns before it grabs you is the ultimate boss move.

Leaning out to lean in

The year 2018 would turn out to be a pivotal year for me. I began to have discussions with my superiors, sponsors and mentors about next steps in my career path at the company. It was not exactly the easiest discussion to have. All of them knew that I had completed successfully what I'd come to do at the company; in fact, I had built something brand new on top of the new department that I created from scratch. My team began to win award after award, and even the new concept began to gain recognition before it launched.

I knew my time was winding down there. What exactly could I do next? The logical step would be to go to another business unit and gain some experience in a profit center. Everyone I spoke to understood that I did not want to do more in diversity and inclusion, and corporate communications wasn't doing it for me anymore, either. I'd successfully built a bridge and a robust working relationship with the marketing department in an attempt to integrate all that we did in the realm of D&I. I was speaking more their language than that of the public relations team; and frankly, it was rubbing some of my colleagues the wrong way.

My seven-year-old daughter has discovered Disney's *High School Musical* franchise, and I have to say my favorite song is one called "Stick to the Status Quo" because it completely describes this timeframe in my career. To some, I was coloring outside the lines with this intrapreneurship stuff that addressed breaking down silos across marketing organizations and bringing inclusion top of mind in all of their meetings. I'd even added intrapreneur to my bio, which rubbed someone the wrong way. They'd even asked my boss to help me re-write it. I was using terms like operationalize, and someone just didn't like it.

I was not only becoming increasingly bored, but the sponsorship in my reporting chain diminished since the company reorganized. It was time to take my mentor's advice. So, in tandem, I started to look outside the company for roles that might reveal my value. There were a few different companies that bit hard. One of them was an international hotel chain. The role had a "Global Head of..." title to it, and it would allow me to pull on my hospitality experience in strategic communications.

I would also be tasked with building the team from scratch, and I'd own about 3 brands in the portfolio. We reached the point in the interview process where it was time to talk about money, and I learned that I could double my cash take-home simply by making a move to Atlanta. Do you know what knowing that did to my psyche? The environment I was in at work was becoming toxic.

That rewrite of my bio was a classic microaggression, ordered from above in a way that would no doubt put me in my place. However, reaching outward and learning my market value allowed me to put it all in perspective. When and if the time came to leave, I could with all the confidence in the world.

I also heard from a former client that had moved on to an incredible position in a totally different industry. She had an SVP of Brand and Communications role that she wanted to speak to me about. I met her at the *Black Enterprise* Women of Power Summit over coffee to talk money and position description. I wasn't clear on timing or if it would actually come to fruition, but it was enough with the hotel chain conversation to prepare my letter of resignation and place it on my desktop. Let's face it: some people do vision boards. I wrote a resignation and pinned it to my work computer. That was my vision: to move on. It was around that time that my contributions for *Black Enterprise* began to really stack up. Looking at the entire body of work, I called a friend who had a web design business. I told her that I wanted a place on the web all my own that housed all my content. A website would be great, not a blog. It would be something where anyone could easily find everything I published, and every bit of media coverage I'd received in the past two years could be found in one place. It would be my birthday present to myself. While she got to work, I continued to speak all over the country on behalf of the company brand. Then one day, a call came through to me that would shift my perspective forever. A representative from the National Association of Black Journalists (NABJ) called. She was planning the program for the next convention in Detroit. She invited me to moderate the opening technology plenary at the convention, the largest gathering of journalists of color in the world. I was stunned. I'd get to work alongside the anchor from ABC Nightline, but I needed clarity. Was she requesting me or was she requesting me as a representative of my company? Without hesitation, she said, "We want you." Now, this wasn't strange. I first joined NABJ when I was 18 and a freshman at Texas Christian University. This was about like my pastor calling me to speak at my church. This was home. It felt right. Why would I not do it? But there was this one outstanding question. How would they refer to me if I wasn't there representing my company? Then I realized how dumb I sounded.

I was a contributor for *Black Enterprise*. I already had a platform. It was time to use it. When I arrived in Detroit, my web designer began sharing the first wireframes of the website. I had secured my URL earlier. It was really coming to life, but something was missing. It was at that moment that I was on the phone with her that the biggest news of the year flowed from my lips: "Summer, I think my site needs something else, and it isn't a blog. It's a podcast. I need to expand my reach and reset my personal brand, and this will be the way I'll do it. I'm giving myself 45 days to launch it. I'll share the name with you soon so that I can have it ready for you when we launch on my birthday, but the show won't launch until Oct 28."

All of this was just the outlet I needed while I was navigating foolery on my floor. At this point, I received a brand new manager who had half my experience in the industry, and was quick to eliminate every speaking opportunity that came my way. He also noted my "potential" in a meeting with dozens of my team members. They were livid. Mind you, he was just doing as he was instructed: take over authority and run the diversity & inclusion corporate communications team. But boy, was it annoying. The most annoying part, besides my having to show him what to do, was that it was a Black man whom I otherwise liked until then. (We'll explore more about how people of color can also act in bias, feed into the power center's agenda and do the dirty work for them later.)

With this new environment, it became crucial that I made a clear distinction between speaking invitations I received as a representative of my company and those that were not related to my 9-to-5. The number of those began to increase. So I dove headfirst into a color story and color theory. That would do the trick, and I'd never need a word to explain it. When I wore bright yellow, so different from my company's brand, I was doing my business. It would be as simple as that. With my value proposition clearly defined, it was a cinch to launch the podcast in no time. "The Culture Soup Podcast®", named for one of the hooks in one of my popular keynote messages, was born. Careful to navigate any compliance issues that could have raised up to bite me, I found a fruitful way to distract myself from the nonsense at work, do some incredible work to reposition my brand and open up some additional streams of income. I had to look for the positive in the situation. Five years of work, albeit great work,could no longer overshadow the 20 years of excellence I'd accomplished before that time.

no silos communications llc became a reality, and it provided me with an extra dose of security whether I stayed at the company or took a position outside of it. It was definitely a value and personal brand booster, inside my company and out. I called myself an extrapreneur. Ironically, a prominent officer applauded me for the work I was doing outside the company at the start of a meeting for women of color; she asked if I were building an off-ramp. I told her, "No." I think she believed me, but you must know that the traditional corporate mindset sees these activities as a desire to leave. This officer has an entrepreneurial spirit herself, launching her own blog and nurturing a vibrant online presence on social media. She understood when I shared that the objective was to expand my reach because I was beginning to write books. I was actually pretty pleased she raised it in front of a room full of women of color. In fact, I loved the fact that she was so open about it, and I had no problem being equally as transparent. It's much better than the undercurrents and whispers from other places.

Watching your back while you do the work

There are a few "watch-outs" for those of you who are planning moneymaking ventures outside of your current 9-to-5. It's great to do both. It's advisable to put your eggs in more than one basket, but here are some of the lessons I learned.

Commit to it and know everyone won't like or understand it. You have to move forward anyway. My mentors and sponsors assured me of this. It may seem like I made these moves in a vacuum, but my tribe was aware of every step and advising me along the way.

Plan and plot, but keep the plans close. Everyone shouldn't know what you're doing. It isn't their business. You don't want to get into the habit of asking permission for the life you are living outside of work. The people you share with should have a vested interest in you and your mission and be able to advise you or support your efforts. When and if you share, do so knowing that everyone may or may not be aligned.

Know the rules and play by them. There is something called compliance. Every company has these guidelines. They are not to be taken lightly. At my company, the rule was not to offer the same work for other entities that you were paid to do there. My business was focused on leadership and career advice, as I would launch "The 30 Minute Mentor" in January of 2019.

Be aware of the unwritten rules, and navigate them like a fox. I mentioned the political craziness that was brewing on my floor because of the unprecedented change that the company was going through. New leaders were making up rules as we went along and dismantling everything my original boss and I had established. By this time, I was absolutely exhausted. You couldn't convince me, at this point, to fight to stay on the road speaking as much as I had been. I had a small child at home with whom I wanted to be with more as she navigated school. I wasn't getting paid to speak in the first place. So my system was this: while the speaking invitations kept coming, my manager needed to know that there was demand for the company message on diversity and inclusion as it pertained to strategic communications. He needed to know that there was an opportunity for the company to shine. So I would share the opportunities that came my way, knowing full well that I had no desire to do them and that they had no desire to allow me to take them. My manager would either shoot them down or pretend as if he pursued approval but never did, and the opportunities would die. I knew at that point that those last- minute declines were doing more to hurt the company's brand than mine, and I welcomed the extra time at home with my little one. Workplace challenges like these really rest squarely on the mindset you decide to take. Understand that your brand has its own value, and your company needs that value to reach audiences it could not reach on its own. Some may accuse you of using their platform to broaden your brand even when your message is clearly about theirs—that's gas lighting, another form of microaggression. Allow your tribe to center you and tell you the truth. Your brand has value; and your speaking, social sharing and other forms of employee advocacy actually come at a premium. You will more than likely never get compensated for that activity. You're literally saving your company marketing budget when you post on social media or speak for free on their behalf, and they are not paying an influencer to do the same advocacy.

Always find the message in the mess. Political nonsense in the workplace can take a toll on you. You will go through; however, I've heard more than one preacher say that there is always a message in the mess. It's our job to look for the positive opportunities and move forward with those. In my case, a negative situation proved to be the thing that would tee up my ability to build my value in the marketplace and inside the company. If you stay with your authenticity, excellence and integrity, you will ultimately win. Naysayers always look for the irrelevant and petty ways to try to pull you down, diminish you or "put you in your place." I frequently ask my clients, "What can you learn from this negative situation that you can use to get to your goal?" I discovered my market value during this trying time, carved out a viable business and learned resilience in the face of adversity. I never will forget the many people who said to me during that time that I carried myself with grace, and that my posture during that time was amazing. When you know who you are and Whose you are, it's simply what you do. Know the difference, and keep shining, Sis.

No one goes at it alone.

As you take on bias in the workplace, it's critical for you to have allies and sponsors who will speak to your character and your value. Every challenge isn't your battle to fight. Sometimes you need to have those critical advocates in other departments and in leadership or in other adjacent industries who will stand up and fight for you, even when you're not in the same room. A great way to be your own best advocate is to intentionally assemble your tribe. It's important for you to weigh out the risk and the reward of staying where you are or stepping off the road and cutting a new path. A powerful, effective and activated tribe is a wonderful way to weigh the options. Some call this the Personal Board of Directors. Whatever you chose to call it, ensure that you've got the right people in the right places who can help you win your battles before they become overwhelming. You should have a group of people around you who will be your sanctuary and provide you a safe harbor for the emotional challenges of rising up the corporate ladder.

Actually assembling your tribe and activating it remains a mystery to many who've also picked up on this pat career advice from experts and books that never quite reveal how to do it. Here is the model I provide to my clients: think of it as a pyramid. It is based on the idea that your network, at the bottom of the pyramid, is the broadest pool of your benign contacts. Your network makes up the foundation of this model. You may have a solid rapport with this group. Once nurtured and a real relationship is forms, they become a part of your community, which is the next level up on the pyramid. These are people you actually know, and they know you and your work. They will also act on your behalf, small everyday gestures, not necessarily in grand ways. You are also willing to do the same for them. Photofy CMO Ted Rubin often says it this way: "Your network is your reach. Your community is your power." He is right.

At the peak of your pyramid is your tribe. These are your "ride-or-die" community members, but they have distinctions. They are not all the same. Before we discuss who they are, let's delve a bit deeper into rapport building, because it all starts there.

In order to build your tribe, networking is a necessary evil, but let's be honest. Not everyone is fond of the idea of meeting someone cold. So how do you optimize a brief meeting, especially in the age of Coronavirus when chances are the meeting will be a virtual one or by phone? It's fairly daunting when your chance at a face-to-face is zero. How do you even set a remote meet-and-greet? Five minutes may be all the face time you get to establish a rapport — the very beginnings of a relationship. However, it is the very foundation of strong ones. In many ways, networking is like dating — the relationship will only take off, if there is mutual interest. #SwipeRight So, how do you spark that interest? Here are five ways to establish a solid rapport for those who identify as introverted. They can even help a die-hard extrovert:

Set your agenda. As with anything, you need to have an agenda — sounds cynical, but you should know exactly what your goal is for your meeting. This is not a talk track. These are items you want to accomplish during your brief encounter. Ask yourself, "What do I want to get out of making this new contact?" Answer that, and crystalize it in your mind. You need no more than 2-3 items on your agenda. In the age of social distancing, you might request a quick Zoom meeting or even a phone call (remember those?).

Raise a question. Consider a leading question at the top of your agenda that will show your new contact that you are familiar with and have an interest in what they do. But that question should also lead you down a path that makes your next step seem natural. Example: "I read your last thought leadership piece on XYZ. I loved that you took a position on ZYX. What do you think about [insert something organic to the topic that will tee up your mission/interests/value]?" A Harvard study has found that there is a link between asking a question and likeability. Be sure to genuinely listen to the answer and ask a follow-up question or engage with the answer in some way.

Share your mission. Some of you have been coached on how to deliver a great elevator pitch. Remember, your "one thing," your value proposition? Your mission adds a little more. Your mission shares your value proposition and the forward motion and the big picture goal that you have for yourself. Again, it is bigger than a title or a job description, and it allows your contact to see your potential. When you share this mission statement, be certain to project confidence.

Call them to action. Invite them to visit your blog, your LinkedIn page, or to meet again. This is your time to lead them on a path to get to know you after your brief meeting ends.

Follow up. Your meetings are only as good as the follow-up you give it. Whether it's a phone call, an e-mail, or a LinkedIn connection, you want to ensure that your follow-up is meaningful to your connection and not simply self-serving. Consider sharing an article that may be of shared interest to kick off a thoughtful exchange, even electronically.

"Un-networking" for those who hate the thought of the other word

Now that you've learned a great way to establish a rapport, it's time to start actually networking. Here are five things you can do, if you absolutely don't like the idea of it. I get it. Some of us are more gregarious than others. Still, others of us shy away from being one of a few or the only one in a setting. Now that social distancing is the norm until we get control of this pandemic, these tips will come in very handy.

About three years ago while working at the big corporation, I received a call from an officer's chief of staff (CoS), inviting me to speak to her mentoring circle about networking. Now if you are like me, I shun the idea of classic networking. I believe that I have something in my DNA that is just simply diametrically opposed to the idea.

I just wasn't built for it. I'm certain it works for some because people continue to push the idea. A popular personality assessment reveals that while I am indeed an extrovert, I have highly introverted tendencies. I really don't like the idea of entering a room full of people that I do not know and striking up conversations that I feel can only be superficial at best.

Some people make excuses for not networking. Some of the most popular ones, according to The Career Experts blog, are that people fear rejection, they aren't comfortable talking to people they don't know, or they simply just don't know how to do it. My approach to networking is a little different, so I shared five tips for that mentoring circle that have worked for me over the years.

Slay everyday. No need for embellishments here: this tip really is focused on performance. While it is important to look your best because first impressions can make or break you, you must complete each and every task or assignment with excellence. In other words, kill it every time, whether the initiative is big or small. Every. Single. Time. This is how good reputations are built and positive buzz about you is created inside and outside of your company. In other words, let's give them something to talk about. Your inability or competency should never be on the table for discussion. The chance for a mutual spark between you and the new connection will be higher. This will increase the chance to create good buzz about you. This is a personal brand building moment that is a small, everyday interaction. Make it count.

Be attractive. This isn't about the outward appearance as much as it is about ensuring that your good reputation precedes you and your personal brand is well-executed so that people want to meet you and know more. There is science behind the rules of attraction. In fact, being available as a resource in business is extremely attractive, according to some research. That same research says that you can't be boring, which means you must be memorable. Our discussion in the mentoring circle centered around the difference between brand and reputation. Your brand is what you put out into the universe proactively. These are the things that you want people to know about you. Your reputation is what people say about you when you aren't in the room. Both can attract people to you or do the exact opposite. Take an assessment of what makes your brand a good one. Consider what is said in rooms where you are not. Do the two things add up? Is there some tweaking to your brand that may impact your reputation? Slaying every day will help.

Leverage social media. If you want to blow off that 8-minute networking event, how about spending more time on platforms like LinkedIn that actually provide you with a way to engage and connect with people without being too bold too soon? In this case, LinkedIn is your friend, and there are stealthy ways to engage without being too "out there." The algorithm makes this really, really simple. Every engagement affords you extended reach. So try liking content that someone in your network shared. Your entire network will see it, but be deliberate about it. Is the content aligned with your brand? Then, yes, give it a thumbs up. If you want to get a little more out there, try commenting. You don't have to post updates or even provide long-form posts to shape your positioning. Engagement can take you places and create connections that you may not have even considered. The ultimate compliment to your community members on LinkedIn is sharing their content on your page. Tag them while you are at it. Then watch your reach expand to not only your network but theirs, as well. Their positive response won't hurt either. By the way, if you haven't given a thought to your digital footprint, you should. Ask yourself, "What do people see when they Google me?" Then be proactive about shaping those search results based on your one-sentence value proposition. *FairyGodBoss* suggests sharing great articles online that may be applicable to the person you'd like to network with or inviting them into your Slack community.

Build a community. So we're back to the idea of community. Let's examine why a community can offer you so much prowess. Communities gather around shared values, and very loosely, as it is extremely obvious in social media, shared content. And those connections are made stronger by the conversations these people have about topics with which they all align. This implies that your community has more than just a passing knowledge of you. Your network may be familiar with you, but your community will vouch for you. So, start with the people you already know, the people who already know your work. The people who you know will actually answer when you call. Start here, and see where it gets you.

Re-enforce that rapport. A rapport is the very beginning of a relationship, and sometimes, a chance meeting or even a planned one can only afford you a few moments to achieve an interaction that can lead to a more fruitful exchange. Solid relationships are how business gets done. I shared the example of how I wound up speaking to the officer's mentoring circle, and it truly demonstrated how the first four tips led to the fifth and ultimately found me speaking in the mentoring circle. The CoS asked the team in Human Resources, Diversity & Inclusion (HR D&I) whom they recommended to speak. HR D&I was one of my clients within the company. I tried to slay all day for them, every opportunity I could. Apparently, it impacted their recommendation. The CoS went to the officer and provided their suggestion and said that she didn't know me.

"You have never heard L. Michelle speak? I have," the officer said. I had been in the room with the officer twice– each time, I was presenting my work. The CoS then turned to LinkedIn, and the post she saw first was the endorsement from my university in the form of 30 billboards across North Texas, and with that, she picked up the phone.

The result of that conversation could have gone another way had the officer said, "You know, I've been in meetings with her, and I really don't think she is a fit." Boom...no invitation. Establishing that rapport initially kicked down a door that may have been shut had I not performed well. But, relationship building isn't simply linear. It's important that you take a 360 approach. Establishing your own board of directors, your tribe, is key to becoming a great leader.

Assembling and activating your tribe

Your story will shape the roadmap to building a great tribe. For me, my story is ultimately an empty narrative without a cast of individuals who has help set my course. I'm talking about my very own board of directors. If I listed their names, they may not mean much to you. Only a couple of them are recognizable or even famous, but none of that matters. What matters is that I can call on them at any time for advice and direction about my career.

There's been a lot of talk lately about having your own board of directors, but those are just buzzwords for having a viable sounding board for career and life matters. And, mind you, this is for those serious about making their way up the career ladder. Some have referred to it as assembling your own "kitchen cabinet," but whatever you call it, here's an effective way to make it happen. In short, do your best work, form solid relationships and let nature take its course.

Your best advocates will come to you. They will recognize something in you, and make the first move. The feeling must be mutual for things to work. Like in dating, it's a really great way to know without a doubt if they have passion about mentoring, sponsoring or advising you. Ultimately, they need to have a passion for maintaining the relationship with you.

Diversity is key. If everyone on your board looks like you, is in the same stage of career, or in the same company or industry as you, start again. There is richness in a collective that can bring a wealth of different experiences and points of view to your journey, and some will be more useful at some seasons in your career than others.

Make new friends, but keep the old. The old Girl Scout song says that one is silver and the other is gold. If you still maintain a relationship with your university professors or thesis chairman, leverage it. Onboard new mentees, but keep up with the ones whose careers have taken off and don't seem to need as much advice. They may have some for you. Former clients from another life are golden. Work your mix and mix your work, and you will profit from it.

Have a platform and a mission. Your board of directors is most powerful when they understand your goals. With that in mind, you'll need to have a crystal-clear understanding of that yourself. If you are mid- to late-career stage, I advise developing a solid platform. It should be one that will solve a business problem and take you into new consideration sets. This is your chance to innovate. Solve a problem that hasn't been solved yet. Leaders literally lead in thought and action. So maintaining your leadership status mandates that you are always looking ahead and solving problems before they even materialize. Your board can support you in this. They will support you in realizing what that can be, see around corners that you can't and help you kick down doors when it's time to make things happen.

Be on someone else's board. It's not all about you. Pour into someone else, and it has a way of pouring right back into you. Have mentees and give them assignments that will cause them to grow. Sponsor someone, and kick down some doors for someone else, perhaps even leveraging your own board.

Coaching questions: What one new step are you willing to take to begin to actively advocate for yourself? What will you commit to in order to begin to intentionally form and activate your tribe? How will you leverage your tribe to navigate the corporate politics and bias?

***

6 "SOME SISTERS HAVE MADE IT TO THE C-SUITE BEING THEMSELVES. I CAN TOO."

Many Black women in Corporate America lit a figurative candle in honor of the retirement of Ursula Burns, the only Black woman to occupy a CEO post in a Fortune 500. She left a chasm so deep and complex, essays were written about it. With her natural hair and no-nonsense straight talk, she was a credible example of taking one's rightful seat at the table. Since then, we've watched the first woman and first Black woman become a CEO in the NBA, Cynthia "Cynt" Marshall, and celebrated. But even she has stories to tell when it comes to microaggressions, successfully climbing, and bringing others with her. Marshall frequently offers sage advice for women in the workplace; encouraging women to #HASU or, "hook a sister up." She recalled her first day in a corporate environment and said she went home that evening knowing she couldn't return with her church shoes, which happened to be red, even though that was really all she had. She frantically told her mother that she had to remove her braids as well because her boss' supervisor told her to do so. They stayed up all night taking them down.

The first Black cheerleader at the University of California, Berkeley, who attended on scholarship because of her engineering skills, knew she was smart; but for some reason, no one cared about all that on her first day at work. They seemed to be focused on the packaging. With Black women noted as the most educated of any group in the U.S., how is it that people in corporate environments seem to get stuck on hairdos and outfits?

It raises the question: can you show up to your corporate job on the first day as your authentic self, as a Black woman, and be taken seriously? That horrifying experience taught the head of the ninth largest NBA franchise something she said she would never forget. You have to deliver your unique magic in doses.

"Yes, you can show up as your authentic self [on day one], but you need to know the playing field, and if your authentic self is going to be risky, and [how] to manage the risk, " Marshall said. She believes that during the interview process, you hope that proper vetting has been done and a good match has been made—that you are a good match for the organization and that they are a good match for you, and I mean all of you.

"But you know what? My advice is: You could just never bring all of you—just ALL of you—in there on day one. At least I know I can't. I know I have a personality that is sometimes larger than life, and I just can't, " Marshall said. "I just have a personality and charisma, so I've been told, and some people don't like all that, because they will misjudge you. They will mistake all the personality for a lack of smarts." Marshall, an engineer by training, used to hide the fact that she loved numbers. She didn't want to be known as a geek. At some point she discovered that was OK, too.

"So it's risky. It's risky," she said. "Just do your homework. Know what that means to bring all of you, and then you make the decision: do you want to bring all of you?" Marshall says that you should exercise your emotional intelligence (EQ) by first understanding the playing field, then when it's "game time" you can bring as much of you as you think is necessary to be in there.

Cheryl Grace has written a book on the subject called *Climbing out of Entry-Level Hell: The Newbie's 12 Steps Up the Career Ladder of Success*. She admits that when she first started her career, she had to find ways to be herself, but at the right times for different audiences.

"When you are first starting a job, it is very important to pay attention to the corporate culture when you are interviewing and understanding that you have a good vibe with that corporate culture. And will you feel comfortable living in that environment every single day? " Grace asked. Grace believes that when you are first starting out, you don't have anything under your belt to say, "I've don't this, this, and this, I can deliver. You haven't done anything yet," she said. "So I do think it is important at the beginning of your career to at least go along with the corporate culture, at least until you can stand on your own successes." Grace believes that once you can stand on your own successes, and not be focused on how you speak or how you dress, they will know that this is the "money person" here. This is the rainmaker, the person who can deliver.

"Until you have that, in my personal opinion, you should get in where you can fit [in] until you can prove yourself. I have a lot of young women who come to me as mentees and say that they are a little more aggressive, that their personality is a little strong. They don't always necessarily understand that this is sometimes cultural. What I've learned is that when I'm in a certain setting, I might lower my voice about it. I'll speak softly about it, because then, they are listening to me, and they are reacting to what I'm saying and not my animation," she said.

"I've learned over the years that since I have such a robust personality that if I want my message to be heard I need to scale it back sometimes for people who may not be used to being around people with robust personalities. I soften my voice. I change my tone, I smile when I talk, and I sit on my hands," Grace said.

Trudy Bourgeois says that you have to have self-awareness. "I worked in politics early on, so I picked up on cues very early on. But, in corporate, as well when I was surrounded by all White men, I knew that it was important for them to hear what I had to say, but I knew that they were not going to listen if they were distracted by the way I was dressed, or by my tone or anything other than my message. I was about halfway through my career and in my 40s when I finally started to understand the impact I could have in a corporate boardroom."

Bourgeois calls this adaptability in the workplace "style flexing." A little less drastic than code switching, she describes it as the ability to bring the tools from your personality arsenal to the table for the right audience at the right time. Code switching or much worse, being someone that you're not, can bring its consequences. But she offered some hope for day-one authenticity. The founder and CEO of the Center for Workplace Excellence believes it can be done, under the right circumstances. "You can show up day one in an authentic way if you bring [your] game. You are a brand; and packaging matters in branding. Packaging matters in marketing," she said. "If you know what you stand for and you know how you want the world to experience you, you show up that way. How you carry yourself does include what you wear. So we have to be mindful that our brands stand for something." Bourgeois says that when we are in a position to demonstrate our brilliance, people will accept us for who we are, but we have to be consistent. We can't cover, and that means we can't pretend to be someone we are not.

"And I did it. I took on male leadership behaviors because I was the only female, the only African American female and I wanted to be accepted. So I figured if I cussed, if I pop a couple of Buds on the golf course, or be 'Ms. Tough-Tough Talk,' that I would be accepted, and indeed I was, but here's the thing that happens," she said. Bourgeois said that one day she looked in the mirror and she didn't know who she was looking at, and she didn't like the person she saw.

"I had to go on my own personal journey to understand what I value and what do I say that I stand for," she said. "Am I showing up in a way that is congruent with my beliefs and values and my desire to have an impact in the world? People can't have that conversation with others until they have had that conversation with themselves. It's about the ability to create your own opportunities by sharing your natural brilliance, and at the same time to be able to style-flex to respond to the needs of your audience, " she said.

You can't be authentic if you don't know who you are.

Sis, I know that you've been told that you can't be yourself in the workplace, but it absolutely is possible to be true to who you are without breaking who you are. Trudy urges women to style-flex without compromising our authentic selves as an intelligent approach to executive presence; however, it's imperative to do the work of knowing exactly who we are and what value we bring. When you are focused on adding value, people will provide you with the space to be who you are. They also need to like who you are in order for them to open doors to the rooms where decisions are being made.

I know, our parents taught us that being respected is more valued than being liked. That's a perspective from another generation, a generation that didn't, for the most part have dreams to be in the C-Suite. Culturally, many of our parents were simply happy to have that "good job" and remain there until retirement. Upward mobility in corporate requires likeability. Your performance is no longer a question when you ascend to this consideration. They want to know who you are and how you will lead. Bourgeois believes that knowing your value and being able to communicate your value proposition not only opens doors, but it creates opportunities that will level the playing field, and in most cases, put you ahead of the pack. She calls it "creating your own equality, and it begins with knowing yourself and being authentic about it. The rest, she says, can lead to seismic change for you, your company, the industry, and sometimes the world. Just think: if we can create our own equality, we can stop thinking that someone else is going to create it for us. We can simply include ourselves because we are attracting the right opportunities consistently.

Your parents were right about first impressions. Let's be realistic. Sometimes people judge simply on what they see and experience with you in a room. Your personal brand begins with visuals.

"In life, we typically dress for the occasion. In the office, the occasion requires that we look professional and pulled-together for the role that we have and the people, clients, or customers that we interact with," said Sheryl Adkins-Green, CMO at Mary Kay.

"Fortunately, today, there are many knowledgeable resources who can help women create a polished professional image; but beyond hair, makeup and fashion, executive presence also includes how one speaks, how one enters the room, how one arranges or decorates their workspace, and more. Everything speaks! We have each been created on purpose, for a purpose."

Green provides advice to women who want to show up to work as their most authentic selves:

1. **Believe in yourself.** If you don't believe in you, why should others believe in you?
2. **Don't try so hard to fit in. It will make you average.** To be extraordinary, you need to celebrate your "extra," not your "ordinary."
3. **Replace doubts with doing. Replace worry with effort**. Stay focused on the role that you can impact.

4. **Comparison is the killer of confidence.** Leverage what makes you "YOU!"

Reasons for authentic leadership that outweigh any reaction you might receive

Authenticity is code for transparency, realness, true diversity that is your own. It opens the doors to many possibilities, but are you willing to own your entire story? If so, the news is good. Authenticity opens the doors to many possibilities and might make the difference between you and the other candidate with all the right credentials and no "it" factor.

People are seeking what is real. In a world of "fakery," people need to find someone who is real, now more than ever. People are questioning everything in their news feeds and on newscasts. Much of it isn't real when you peel back the onion. People claim credentials and expertise they do not have. Some people just, flat out, lie. Be a light. This is your chance to honor what is true by your example.

Authenticity fosters trust. When you are being your truest self, people have very little room to doubt who they are dealing with. Authenticity creates an expectation for fairness and allows access through transparency. Authenticity also makes you more relatable, and people are willing to trust the people that remind them of themselves.

Authenticity distinguishes you from the pack. The higher up the ladder you make it, the field narrows when it comes to smarts and credentials. At some point, everyone may look the same on paper or everyone may be performing at the highest level. Your differentiator is your story and your uniqueness. This is your diversity, and everyone has their own uniqueness.

Authenticity flexes EQ muscle. One of the keys to authenticity is being aware of the environments and those who interact with you. This is your emotional intelligence quotient or EQ. EQ is also about being aware of how they respond to you. When you become proficient in it, you become an excellent leader. Leverage those soft skills!

You will inspire and lead with influence. Gone are the days when aloofness was chic. Miranda Priestly is only celebrated in the movies, and she was lonely. Authentic leadership allows you to share your unique story, journey and lessons learned along the way. Leading shouldn't and doesn't need to be lonely. When you are authentic, you are engaging and inspiring. People will follow you, but not out of fear and obligation but because they want more of what you have to offer—value, inspiration, insight and realness.

Be brave. Do you, not her.
Another behavior that keeps Black women stuck in our own heads is watching other Black women soar then concluding, "If I can just do what she does, I can be a boss." Women who ascribe to this thinking do not fully understand that the woman they admire has claimed her own story and value, mapped her own journey, and bet on her own brand. She is walking in her power and

entitlement as a daughter of God, surrounding herself with an able and extraordinary tribe that pours into her and knocks down doors for her. Then she boldly moves forward even when challenges present themselves. These sisters are brave!

This is the work. How many of you will really commit to do this internal work? Charting your own path has little to do with pat career advice you may receive from the business experts and media and even less to do with how your managers and coworkers act. The rest is up to you. Many decide to stay right where they are because it seems safer.

Still, many women obsess over the journeys of others, scouring their LinkedIn profile and updates, combing their resumes, binging on their social newsfeeds to see what they might do to replicate every perceived step they take.

Sis... *STOP*. Osmosis won't work. "Manifesting" it by obsessing about your role model won't either. There is no magic bullet. So, if you are determined to stay "safe" you definitely won't get to the C-Suite. Rockstar leaders run to the risk. They lean into courage and they chart their own path. Yes, admire someone's journey, but understand you cannot replicate it. It isn't yours. Do the work. Understand your story, the good and the bad. Shift your mindset. Write your own story; know that you are entitled to every good thing because you exude excellence. Then watch yourself become unstuck.

If we all believed that it was our birthright to have and enjoy the same things that others do, it would at least add some additional pep to our step. At the most, it will help us crash the C-Suite or go after our wildest dreams without hesitation.

Coaching questions: What scares you the most about being all you in the workplace? What can you do about how you show up that can help overcome that fear?

***

Affirmation 6:

7 "I WILL BET ON MY BRAND."

What problem do you solve? Can you answer that question? If you answered with a particular hard skill or referenced your job title in any way, try again to answer the question understanding what value you bring. The one-sentence answer is the North Star for your personal brand. This is your *value proposition*. Too often people simply conflate social media presence with personal brand, but there is far more to it than that.

It is also difficult to know what problem you solve if you can't determine whom you solve it for. Clarity around your target audience, as we would say in marketing, is crucial to uncovering and developing your value proposition. In order to bet on your brand, you must know what that brand is and what value you bring. All of this is embedded in your story, and the work that you've done so far as you've continued in this book. This is the work that will begin to unravel key components to personal branding.

Also, integral to your brand is how you want people to feel when you engage with them. Work backwards, and you can begin to be intentional about how you engage with the people you encounter. Stop for a moment and reflect on what it feels like to be a customer at Nordstrom. This is the brand that is known for its incredible customer service. That didn't just happen. Scores of professionals gather in rooms everyday to plan ways to maintain their brand positioning over time, despite changes in the environment.

I know that I feel catered to when I walk into one of their stores, or even when I order shoes from their user-friendly app. Nothing can beat the feeling of Christmas anytime when those boxes arrive at my door. I smile so big and giggle a bit. Even my seven year old gets jealous. While you are neither a big retailer, nor a tube of toothpaste, there are lessons we can take away from the consumer brand professionals that do branding the right way everyday and make millions and billions doing it. Sis, if you are going to do it, you might as well do it right, no? So for a moment, hold back on the temptation to begin posting updates on social media all of a sudden, and let's work through your "why." You want to be a leader, an executive leader. You have C-Suite goals. Let's talk about what that journey requires and who needs to engage with you to make that happen.

The importance of fine-tuning your "one thing"

You must get your "one thing" right. Your one thing is the value you bring when you show up. This one thing must be clear because research says that you only have 7 seconds to make a good impression. It takes 5-7 impressions to create awareness, so your one thing must be translatable to every platform where you show up. That means beyond social media, it needs to be apparent in boardrooms and team meetings. I call these the small, everyday, yet meaningful engagements. It also needs to be apparent in your grand gestures. These are your speaking engagements, your media interviews, your social media posts, those things that can set you apart as a thought leader in the industry and not simply your company.

It follows that you must be able to articulate your "one thing" concisely, because it must be digestible, simple. Cruise LinkedIn headlines, and it will be apparent that this is not common knowledge. You have three camps: the professional that posts their job title, the person who lists everything they have ever done or want to do with all the flowery language they can muster and fit into 140 characters, and the personal branding pro that states their value in one, concise and understandable sentence.

Here is a simple formula to follow:

I help X to do Y with/through/by Z.

I saw one on LinkedIn that followed this exact template. It said something similar to this:

I help coaches to scale their businesses to 6 and 7-figures with proven video funnel strategies.

This is the value proposition, the one thing. To improve upon this, consider the current cultural and business context, so that you can sync with the moment in time. It is also important to speak to one person instead of millions. People want to see themselves in what you offer, so you want to speak to their pain points in a way that they would say it. An example could be this:

I help coaches to scale their businesses to 6 and 7-figures with proven video funnel strategies despite downturns.

With your value proposition developed, you're set to begin mapping out your content and content delivery strategies. Now, before I go all the way in on the marketing terms, let's begin with the small, everyday, meaningful interactions, perhaps, your email correspondences, your team meetings and your work product. Think of three words that describe the way you want people to feel or what we call in strategic communications, "the take away." Perhaps you want the people you interact with to feel a sense of excellence, strategy and warmth. So in an email, this can translate into being concise and to the point, thoughtful and always big picture-focused; and finally, there are implications for your salutations and signature.

Simple shifts like these can completely reposition someone who has been viewed as a tactician or executer to a consultative resource with vision. That, my Sister, is a step in the right direction to executive leadership. Sometimes we get so caught up in doing our jobs just right, over delivering on projects that we forget to raise our heads and merchandise our thinking. By the time you are being considered for an executive leadership role, the idea of "can she do the job each day" is an afterthought. The leaders making those decisions begin to differentiate the talent with other criteria, softer skills that motivate and influence people to move, think and act differently. Once you know what they are looking for, it's time to ensure your value proposition meets those very desires. With the hard work out of the way, it's time to think about how and when you will deliver those grand gestures for your brand.

Making employee advocacy a win-win

Within the past several years, companies have adopted digital employee advocacy as a way to harness the power of their workforce for low-cost, high-impact marketing, sales, and recruiting. But if you are an employee, you may be questioning whether your quest to be loud and proud for your company conflicts with your goal of building your personal brand.

When you first tweeted in 2009, you began to piece together a following that may predate your time at your current job—including those LinkedIn contacts; classmates from your alma mater; and relationships that span the gamut of your professional existence. Your Facebook page is a virtual backyard barbecue that includes, in some cases, people with whom you even went to elementary school. Are they really that excited to hear about your company? Your networks are your currency. Your social platforms are your real estate. They have value, and your company recognizes this. Do you?

Now, consider again if you have allowed the employee advocacy movement to come into conflict, or worse, overtake your personal brand real estate, and/or currency.

It is very easy to do. If you work for a company that you are proud of, it doesn't take much to inundate your social networks with your company news and never think twice about it. That digital advocacy platform is just the convenient and gentle nudge you need to deliver your company's expectations. And after all, it is opt-in; it's pretty and user-friendly and takes little to no thought to share. No one is forcing you to post. Right? Here are some of the latest predictions for employee advocacy from Everyone Social, a platform for engaging employees in a company's external social media efforts. Among them, professional use of personal brand handles is surging. That prediction is linked to the idea that the algorithms on popular sites are putting the squeeze on brands, making it tougher for their organic content to be seen unless they fork over a sizeable spend.

Let us also consider the other popular method that brands use to hopscotch the algorithm predicament: influencer marketing. According to recent research, brands are spending billions of dollars with individuals to share their messages, products and services with their communities. Brands engage these influencers to reach niche audiences that they are less likely to reach. A celebrity and even micro influencers would have more access to these groups.

So, companies are beginning to opt for employees as influencers because they only have to pay for the platform itself. Employee advocacy eliminates influencer or talent fees and is essentially next-gen, mini-micro influencer marketing on a budget. Ted Rubin, CMO of Photofy says digital employee advocacy—if brands execute it well—can work for the company and the employee.

"If executed correctly by the brand, and it rarely if ever is, the two can work together to great advantage for both the brand and the employee," said Rubin. "I believe employee advocacy is most often a win for the brand but can be a much bigger long-lasting win, and truly empower employees, if executed to best advantage with employee benefit at the heart."

However, John G. Graham, Jr., employer brand evangelist and diversity, equity and inclusion advocate, warns about sharing company news on your personal social networks. "The promise that I offer to employees who engage in advocacy efforts on behalf of the company is visibility and exposure of their personal brand to broader audiences," Graham said. "Yes, the employer brand is gaining visibility and exposure as a secondary benefit, but the reality is you're raising your profile by adding value to your personal networks via relevant content that resonates. It's really a win-win."

But is personal branding really that important? Experts say now, more than ever, positioning oneself digitally for the next opportunity is paramount, whether it is within your current company or somewhere else. It can be as simple as a powerful summary on your LinkedIn page, or as involved as contributing as a thought leader to a respected publication. Even a blog or compelling micro blogging or social posts can go a long way. And this isn't selfish or self-promotion, despite what some may believe.

Black women are typically categorized this way, when we decide to be intentional about our personal brands, but this is now basic career survival in the digital age. Building your personal brand is also smart. Many companies are right-sizing for digital transformation and shifting to meet consumer and customer demands. Often, these moves can mean surplus. In June 2018 alone, many of the most recognizable brands announced layoffs. The trend will likely continue as more automation like artificial intelligence takes over. Graham suggests employee advocacy and personal branding can and should co-exist, but employee advocacy extends past social platforms through speaking opportunities and other spokesperson opportunities. He travels the world sharing how it should work.

Graham warns against employees sharing company content through their personal profiles, for a two reasons: Your network isn't that interested in your company if the content you're sharing isn't relevant to their own personal interests. It's also viewed as disingenuous and inauthentic. So, can a company hurt your chances of actually effectively leveraging your own social media capital for your career advantage with broken employee advocacy programs? Does it create a culture of expectation from peers and even superiors that if you aren't sharing company news, you are not "all-in" for the company? Can it cause colleagues or bosses to criticize posts that are solely about your career interests, thoughts, and aspirations? Do these company initiatives create unreal expectations for their employees to leverage their social capital for nothing in return? Dare we ask, is this exploitation? Graham says that employees can and should take control of their social handles, social equity, social media currency, communities and networks. Doing so can also benefit your company. He says employer brands should provide shareable digital content that will add value to the employee and their personal networks. Otherwise, companies risk jeopardizing the very trust their employees have established with their own social networks.

"Leveraging the employee network as a means of extending company content reach and engagement, in my opinion, only benefits the company at the potential risk of the employee networks being turned off by corporate exploitation," he said. "Instead, companies should seek to curate value-add content that their employees can share so as to be more credible and valuable to their networks." He adds, "Doing so ensures that if and when their employees share company-related content, their networks are more apt to engage with it because they've proven themselves trustworthy and a reliable source of content worth engaging with in the past."

Rubin shared advice on how brands can provide content that actually engages your employee's social communities instead of turning them off with commercialism. For example, set some formal guidelines, but stay fluid. Rubin says that if companies clamp down too hard on employees they may simply back away from participating. Train them, then crowd source.

"Offer in-house social training, led by your best in-house (but only if you really have them) and local experts," said Rubin. "Consider offering incentive programs. It can be something as simple as public recognition, but reward those employees who provide the most relevant ideas and responses on how best to empower them to build and leverage their personal brands."

Remember that your employees are your company's best resource. Rubin says to make the most of employee passion and individuality. "Provide content that helps them become experts, leaders, and go- to resources, he said. "They're already social, so start thinking of how you can empower your employees to have their own voice, and you will discover many can, and will, become your company's most active and valuable social advocates."

You are an influencer, so what will you do about it?

So now that you know you are one of your company's most valued influencers, it is time to act like it. Here are three steps that I learned while building strategic communications plans for some familiar brands. They might help you navigate this brave new world of corporate employee advocacy while managing and growing your personal brand in the digital space.

Tip the scales in your own favor. Your company is great. They are doing wonderful things in the community. Awesome. They also have a marketing spend that dwarfs your own. In fact, you likely don't have one. Engage the 80:20 rule. Maybe you can't resist sharing about your company, or feel the pressure to from colleagues, dare I say, bosses to share company news. About 80% of your social media shares should be for your thought leadership. Spend time crafting a deliberate approach to delivering rich and useful content for your community that will benefit them. If a social share from your company aligns with your passions and brand and provides useful content, share it. For example, the share might be tips and advice on career and leadership. Whatever you do, resist alienating your community members. Remember that they would rather see more relatable content in their newsfeeds. Most often, relatable content would consist of your ideas and useful shares that have meaning to you and by extension, them. After all, they are following you, not your company. If they want to follow your company, they can do that.

Have an informed point of view. Opinionated posts that aren't grounded in data that have become the norm   on Facebook do not reflect an informed point of view. Informed posts are research-driven and reflect a seasoned worldview concerning your industry and your business. Focus your content and shares on this sweet spot. Again, if company content aligns with your informed point of view, then share that too, but in moderation.

Guard your social media real estate. It is precious. Don't just give it away. Understand that it is the one place you have to add your unique value, tell your story, and tell it well. Have a deliberate approach that focuses on no more than three broad topic areas that align with your brand and execute against it methodically. Spend some time thinking about your purpose, and it will be apparent to your networks, recruiters, and prospects. Your job is a part of that story, but be careful not to make it the headline. Most of the mishaps that I see with professionals on social media happen on LinkedIn. Most professionals agree that LinkedIn is the place you should be to do business online and to be visible. I've heard this from the clients and audience members at the multiple events and conferences where I've spoken and even from colleagues. It amazes me, however, how many of these professionals simply don't engage on the platform. They set up their page, their "about" section, and then they either rarely visit it again or lurk. I figured there were reasons, however, and I endeavored to find out why.

So you hate LinkedIn. You aren't alone.

Some of you have said it before: "...but I don't want to be out there, you know?" To which I respond, "But do you want to be found?" That is the real question.

Here are many of the reasons professionals tell me they fear, and in some cases, downright loathe posting on LinkedIn:

1. My colleagues and bosses are there—watching and judging me.
2. I don't know what to say.
3. I do know what to say, but have virtual stage fright.
4. I'm not an "influencer," so why would I try to sound like one?
5. I don't believe I'm outgoing enough.
6. How will I sustain it?

7. I don't have time.
8. My peers don't do it, so why should I?
9. I'm not looking for a job right now, or I'm happy where I am.
10. What if I say something dumb?
11. I'm not currently at a company—what would I say?
12. I'm introverted. I'd need to be more extroverted.
13. I'm not a blogger. Should I be?

Can you relate to any of these? It's time to get out of your own way and wield what is your very on social media real estate. It's crucial that you do so in a way that will benefit you and your company so that you can move to the next level of executive influence.

There really is more to social media than event photos, "ussies," corporate hashtags, group shots on a step and repeat, "food porn," vacations and party pictures; but how do you unlock the kind of content that attracts and inspires the people you are really after, like new clients, strategic alliances, industry peers and new opportunities? I learned this first-hand, and it was a bumpy ride, but worth it. I literally had to shift my content, my followers and my channels across my social media mix to begin to attract the right people—people who wanted to hear my message and hire me; people who were inspired by the message I shared and who wanted to secure my services or purchase my products; people who were in my target audience. These probably aren't your current colleagues, your bosses, or even your family or friends. These are the people who actually need the value you have to offer: the thought leadership, the services, the products and the business connections you may offer. If you've noticed that your followers are a little uncomfortable with your attempts at a new direction, it's time to get your content and channel strategy aligned with your goals. For others of you, you've isolated your entire network because you constantly post about your employer's brand.

Then again, maybe you haven't, because your entire social network works at the same company. In any case, you need a change. You may want to be more effective on your platforms, be authentic and engage yourself instead of leaning into the cookie-cutter approaches of your well-intentioned corporate communications support. Maybe you are confused about whether you are being too much   of an influencer and not enough of a business leader online.

If you want to be a better leader, become a business leader who is fluent in social media as a tool, a weapon of mass innovation. Social media can unleash the crucial potential to broaden your leadership footprint beyond the room where you stand, the company where you work. Rockstar leaders get this. This is your executive digital presence, and it is crucial. Wield the right kind of influence and win—light up your direct messages (DMs) with the business deals that matter. That is where the real business happens. This is serious business.

The secret weapon you already have that should be an intentional part of your brand

I use the metaphor of a basket to describe the concept of a brand, personal or otherwise. You have the ability to be intentional about what you place in the basket or take from it. Your personal brand really is the experience you want others to have with you in life. Work is a part of that. How you amplify that experience will create brand awareness. That's what the interrelationship between brand and social media really is.

I encourage my clients to ensure that their offline experience is intentional and aligned with how they want to show up. If you get that right, it is easier to build brand loyalty, which is ultimately what we as leaders should be after. These are the people who are attracted to you and follow you, not in the social media sense, but in the leadership sense. They follow you because their experience with you is exactly what they need, and it is not only a pleasure, but an inspiration. Execute your brand impeccably, and you can create demand for the problem you solve.

Take some time to think about how you are leveraging your EQ for your brand. Experts tout the importance of EQ as essential to great leadership, and it's true. Reading the room, ones you are in or not, and how you interact with the people in it, is an important skill. At the core is empathy. The leader who is willing to walk in the shoes of those that she leads is crucial and separates managers and bosses from the rockstars.

Black women who are high-performing and

credentialed typically have a varied experience in society, interacting with people from all sorts of backgrounds whether from their work experience or during their time in a university setting, international travel or beyond; however, nothing compares to that one experience we all share—being the only one in the room.

Cultural Intelligence Quotient (CQ) amps up the empathy, which is core to EQ, allowing you to understand and walk in the shoes of people of other cultures. EQ and IQ are nothing without CQ. Bringing that superpower to the table is absolutely game changing. Cultural insight is a key weapon you can count as a part of your brand arsenal, especially during times of change and incredible upheaval in the areas of social justice and even through the pandemic. It's an advantage that underrepresented professionals have over their more privileged counterparts because we know what it is like in the margins. Many White colleagues have to work a little harder to level up their CQ because being centered typically finds you in a place of advantage and privilege with little knowledge of what it is like to be marginalized.

I remember a time when I was managing about five different agency teams, each representing a separate culture. One of those teams was Asian American. This amazing team bore distinctive cultural nuances, many of them relatable to me as a woman of color. Others were not. You see, Black women, Asian Women, Latinas and others of color have challenges in the workplace. We've established that. All three are frequently underestimated and often expected to take a more subservient role in corporate settings—remembering again that White maleness is centered—we are all outsiders times two. That said, an aspect of Asian culture that is different from Black culture is the premium placed on avoiding conflict. Asian women are also arguably more invisible in the decision-making realm because of this, unless they buck the stereotype, which is a great way to become marked as a troublemaker both by your culture and by the power structure. Speaking up for yourself is definitely something that isn't smiled upon in the Asian culture, traditionally, and especially from a gender perspective. Times are changing, however.

Combine that with how Asian women are viewed in the corporate fabric, and it's complicated. Asian Americans, in general, are beginning to push back on the "model minority" stereotype that is meant to separate and elevate them from Black and the LatinX communities which are consistently stereotyped as less able to "achieve the American Dream" without the help of the government. Although there appears to be a gap in research concerning this, from my experience, dealing with conflict straight-on is actually a cultural asset in the Black community, so much so that it is typically stereotyped in the media. You know, the strong, neck-rolling, finger-snapping Black woman who "snatches wigs and edges" on everything from modern-day reality TV back to the heavy-handed, overweight mothers that harken to the mammy image of slave times. It's a signature caricature of the late 70s and early 80s television era.

Latinas can't avoid the stereotype either. Caricatures are too numerous to name. She is the fiery, triggered and emotional woman in tight, colorful clothing who launches into Spanish-language tirades at the drop of a hat. Fortunately, there is a grain of truth in every stereotype. Remember stereotypes are a gross exaggeration of the truth. The truth is that highly polished, corporate Asian-American, LatinX and Black professionals know how to channel the best parts of their culture to amazing results.

Now, I share this next anecdote with some degree of caution. Making room for personalities and temperaments, know that some cultural nuances are indeed generalizations. It is very possible to be a Black woman or Latina who avoids conflict, but knowing what I knew about my team members and colleagues, this was one time I could engage the nuances with extreme confidence. What I did in this instance is not advisable for cultural novices. But as over-credentialed, well-traveled, well-socialized (with other cultures) and seasoned women of color, we have advanced-level CQ. To others, decisions like these could be like presenting a loaded Uzi to a toddler. Be advised.

I made a decision one day that would support both my Asian agency and engage and simultaneously uplift a cultural competency of my Black team member, whose role was to liaise with and manage the Asian American agency. One day over lunch he learned that one of the client contacts on the West Coast was being extremely heavy handed with the agency team members. It was so bad, that team members were quietly in tears, others were quitting; but no one on the team would speak up. That is, no one but one agency team member, a young woman who took a risk and confided in my team member about the issues privately. He brought the situation to me because he didn't understand why the agency members wouldn't simply stand up for themselves. I explained to him the nuance in Asian culture to avoid conflict, and he became angry and sad at the same time.

"What can we do?" he asked, himself a member of the LGBTQ community, who had multiple stereotypes to navigate on the daily because of his own otherness. But I had a plan. I asked him to be on every client call with this particular colleague and the agency. Whenever he sensed that the abuse was starting, I instructed him to engage, but I said it to him under my breath the way I absolutely meant it:

"Be as Black about this as you want to be," I said. "You mean I get to gather her up, professionally, of course?" he asked.

"Yes, indeed. You need to stand in the gap for our Asian team members and document what is happening. Then I will take it to her manager and this whole thing will stop." My team member did just that, and he began to see a marked difference in the way the agency felt and performed their work. They stopped quitting and were incredibly grateful for the intervention. The kicker? The client contact that was being heavy handed was also Asian American, and she was well aware of what she was doing. I also knew that sharing the issue with her Latina manager would quickly merit corrective action. Insight into the

LatinX culture nearly guaranteed it as well. In general, my Brown sisters are fearless when dealing with conflict. Conflict management is core to great leadership. I knew we could work this out for the good of my Asian American agency team members, and not one of us raised our voices.

We don't have to.

Within weeks, all was well. People were smiling again, and the work was getting done excellently and at an amazing clip.

Coaching questions: What one step are you willing to make to begin to build your personal brand to support your leadership goals? What will you do to communicate your "one thing" in a powerful and meaningful way? How will you engage your CQ to innovate?

***

8 "I WILL TAKE POSITIVE CUES FROM WHITE PRIVILEGE BECAUSE I'M ENTITLED."

That same year, a few of my colleagues and I attended a panel discussion at the yearly diversity conference for employees at the company. There we were. Fine people, fine clothes, fine cars, fine degrees. I'm telling you, we were three smart and well-coifed sisters: over-educated, well credentialed and well-heeled. We fit the corporate stereotype of Black women extremely well, which is not a bad thing at all. However, we found ourselves pondering a couple of the exchanges from the session.

All I can really remember is that we were having the meeting after the meeting. You know, the one where everything that should have been said in the meeting was actually being discussed after the meeting, in the hallway? Now, this next part gets fuzzy before it gets clear again. There were a lot of "uhh-huhs." and "yeah-girls" being said and echoed, and for the life of me, I can't remember the thing I said that led me to say:

"Well, and you know I could never say that." My sister-friend colleagues all said again, "uhhh-huhh." All was well until one of the nicest White, senior officers rolled up on us and said, "Why wouldn't you say it, Michelle? I would say it."

All three of us looked at him, blankly. First of all, this was a caucus of some of the finest sisters in corporate. He was not invited, even though we were in a common space. I turned and looked at my colleagues. We exchanged "the look." Although we all liked this guy, at the moment, he was not a part of this particular dialogue. We were centered for that very moment. In an instant, we were not, again.

"I would say it," he repeated. "And I'll tell you why. What could they do to me but take my job? And you know what? I'd just go find another one."

That part I remember clearly. All three of us were simply silent, and looking at him. In my head, I was saying, "Of course you would, you're a White male, dude." And that is when it hit me: This man was privileged.

He was valued in the corporate space and virtually anywhere in the U.S. He felt the unbridled freedom to say something without fear, and while he knew that what he would have said would have favored under-represented groups and was anti-racist, he was absolutely certain that if his opinion was unpopular and retribution was in store, he would land again successfully, somewhere else, and be happy.

This exchange rocked my world. Why was it that these

three Black women—the picture of poise, beauty, brains, credentials, resilience and know-how—had a sheer fear of speaking up for the greater good and essentially for themselves? Most importantly, though, the last thing that occurred to us was, "I'll just go find another job." How could this be? Our response was that they could take our jobs. Period. End of story. Oddly, I knew all the reasons why, and thanks to some recent studies, I could articulate it with stats.

Reason 1: What Black women believe about the workplace is cultural and generational. We come from a long history of discrimination. In fact, my dad was one of the first Black men to integrate civil service in the computer field here in Texas in the 60s. He learned quickly to do his work and not to kick up too much dust simply to survive. It was about keeping the peace back then, to secure his retirement and pension when it was time. Promotions came when you were tapped on the shoulder, not when you merchandised your own work. Speaking up on topics of equality was just not heard of. Did they even use the word "diversity" in the workplace in the 60s? The word was "integration"' if there was any talk of anything like diversity. MLK was doing enough of that on television, and you pulled for him in the privacy of your own home. And yet, they saw what happened to him. My home church in Dallas was the only venue brave enough to host Dr. King in our pulpit; otherwise, he had no place to go in the city where within a few years, President John F. Kennedy, Jr. would be assassinated. Black people were simply to be happy with the jobs we were given, and we prayed someone would recognize us. If not, we simply prayed we could survive the experience without too many psychological scars.

Reason 2: Black women are afraid. We are fearful because what we feel to be true really is true: Microaggressions, discrimination, racism, bias, unconscious or not, are real. It has always been real to us, but it is finally real to many others who chose to believe it. The fear is real because smart phone and bodycam footage captured murders at the hands of police like George Floyd, or they chronicled stories like Amaud Aubery's. He was gunned down for simply taking a jog through a neighborhood. Black lives and Black livelihoods are intertwined. If we survive on the outside, we bring our Black lives with us into the workplace where our livelihoods are at stake. Virtually, much of the world has joined in to march and protest racism against Black people. Data on what women and women of color, especially Black women, experience day in and day out has now been published year over year since 2017 thank s to McKinsey/ LeanIn.Org and Catalyst Research. Everyone we knew who looked like us had felt it and had stories to share about being a "double outsider" before it even had a name. Now we have panel discussions about it because, well, there it is in black and white. Now the ugly truth is on our social media news streams and talked about during virtual videoconferences and summits.

Reason 3: Black women are not centered in the workplace. If we are valued, we have to bring our feelings of value and worth from home and our communities into the workplace when we walk through the door. Our value won't be affirmed by anyone unless we find that rare moment in the common area at a conference where we can fellowship together. High-ranking Black women are few and far between. If the company is mammoth, chances are you only have informal meetings like these when you have an all-employee event. There is always a chance that someone like us is in senior leadership and intentionally affirms us. You may find as I have that being like us and intentionally affirming is mutually exclusive. The stars must align to have both. Still, there are White leaders who will affirm you. Like our friend in the story, these are White leaders who are so centered in their privilege and aware that they can speak up, that they will advocate for us when given the chance. However, even our friend knew that speaking up could carry consequences, but his response to the idea of the consequence is when I had my "ah-ha" moment. He quickly whipped up a contingency plan, proactively and confidently, which is not what Black women in corporate tend to do. I know. I coach them. I've surveyed this demographic. I have a number of mentees who are Black women. I am one. This is not how we generally think or react to speaking up and advocating for Black people, let alone ourselves, in corporate spaces.

Shifting your mindset to compete in a new and different time

I had to ask myself this question: It was 2018. It probably was not a crazy leap to assume that if the three of us Black women executives with all of our credentials, expertise and fineness had found ourselves in an uncomfortable situation at work that we, too, could simply find another job and life would go on. Why didn't we make that not-so-giant leap in our minds?

Fear had us by our very souls. We were hanging on for dear life in our minds to our positions. It was as if these jobs were the only ones we could ever find. It was as if the world would end if we did not remain in those roles only. If I could time- travel back to 2018, the executive coach in me would ask all three of us, as I now pose to my clients: what has you standing in the way of your own progress? How was your confidence high jacked, even in your high heels, some of them with red soles?

This hesitancy to move forward, out, away is a mindset. It is what I call an analog mindset. An analog mindset is not an entrepreneurial one. It is far from transformational and definitely does not lend itself to this fast-moving digital economy where change is at the center of everything. It's also a fixed mindset, which is the very opposite of a growth mindset as defined by American psychologist Carol Dweck, a professor at Stanford University. A fixed mindset says that if failure happens, in this case, if your job was taken from you for standing up for yourself, that failure defines you. A growth mindset says quite the opposite, that the failure is an incident that happened that you can learn from and move forward despite. So, this analog mindset, which denies the power of the digital age and is fixed, keeps us stuck in less-than-optimal positions in the workplace.

At the very least, the analog mindset leaves us comfortable. Comfortable may sound positive, but remember, the goal is to move up, to move forward. Applied positive psychology shows us that we are rarely growing when we are comfortable. We may be drawing a nice salary every two weeks. We may be taking the yearly trip to some exotic place with the girlfriends so that we can ride on the backs of camels in some far-flung destination, "doing it for the 'gram." We may have the designer bags and clothes and may be having fabulous nights out, money spewing from the tops of champagne bottles.

What is the tradeoff, however? Every year at the annual review, we have to negotiate, no, debate—sometimes verbally scuffle with our managers over a percentage point of an increase and a lump-sum bonus that probably could have been a part of your initial salary package. And yet, your manager continues to dangle that money over your head like a carrot at performance review time.

It's a little crazy that in four short years, I had re-adopted this mindset myself. I knew better. I had run an agency on my own with no co-founder or partner before landing an officer role at a global agency and bringing a couple of accounts with me. Then I ultimately landed at the behemoth company where that encounter with the White male leader happened with my sisters. I'd never had to "look" for a job out of necessity except for right out of undergraduate school and after I closed the agency. Even then, I phoned a few high-ranking executives in the global agency realm. In fact, most of the positions I landed after my first role in PR were results of my looking out of curiosity, checking my market value or someone calling me, not the other way around. I had to remind myself that that is how I landed this particular job in the first place. I was minding my own business with my new baby girl at home, not thinking about a job, when the phone rang and I was told, "We will stop the search if you put yourself forward."

Which leads me to my assertion: If Black women can 'flip privilege' and begin to walk tall like White men in business, we can crash the double-paned Black ceiling and be our unapologetic selves along the way. The key is overcoming the fears.

I became a certified executive and business coach for this very reason—to help my sisters begin to reframe their mindsets, to overcome the mental blockages like fear that are holding us back. I realize that right where we get stuck, in the middle of the leadership pipeline, is about the time that women of color need support like mine, before they bail with little experience and minimal access to capital to start their own businesses. However, sometimes the blockages are, again, cultural, sometimes it is societal. Sometimes it is racial; however, sometimes, it's just us. Another, challenge for Black women stuck in the middle is this: access to resources like professional executive coaches. Many of these huge companies only provide executive coaching services as a perk for the most senior leaders. Mid-level and general managers may never know that executive coaches exist. They could very well brush shoulders with one in the very hallways where they have water cooler conversations and never know. We are just that stealth. So, in addition to organizational coaching, seminars and workshops, I am also the accessible executive coach for individuals who want to retain my services personally and not at the same expense as a Fortune 500 company. Let's face it, access to an executive coach is indeed a privilege.

I recently unpacked the idea of privilege on "The Culture Podcast®" with my friend of some 15 years, Dr. Jeff Gardere, also known as America's Psychologist. He said that there are indeed positive aspects to privilege that under-represented people can take and apply to themselves: *self-love* and *knowledge of self*, an *awareness of one's value* and *the tendency to act boldly.*

What if we could adjust our mindsets, manufacture the value White men innately have in the workplace and beyond? What if we could recreate some of these advantages, and walk without fear of reprisal...or at least with a solid plan in case reprisal does happen? What if we could think like a White man? Could it actually free us up to be our authentic selves, walk in our own power, own our own careers and journeys, run to the risk and innovate without fear of failure?

I practice this, and I have mentors and sponsors who act it out daily in the highest levels of Corporate America. But we have to lean outside of the structure to grasp our entitlement, which is something that many Black women and other women of color are uncomfortable with. In fact, the word corporate, itself, means one body. It's nearly comical that the word diversity can even exist within that concept because it really signifies moving as one, acting as one, being one. The corporate culture resists the notion of being anything but what the corporate culture dictates. And if that culture is centered around White maleness and doing things by the company and for the company all the time, leaning outward and betting on your own brand as a Black woman, is by definition, counter-cultural. It is an act of sheer courage. And yet, this new fractured digital and cultural economy demands it.

Moving forward despite a rigged system I remember growing up in my home church when my pastor, the legendary C.A.W. Clark, preached a sermon called "The Game is Fixed." It was a liturgy of storytelling and metaphors about how God's love, and therefore His children, always win in the end. Black women have to take this victory to heart because this system, business and the corporate workplace were not built with us in mind. It was built to favor people who are not us. While many are working to try to change it, if change comes, it won't be suddenly. That really is how it is, my Sister. Our society is also that way, and there are people of color and other underrepresented groups who are so bought-in to the power structure and the culture of the analog mindset that they will do everything they can to maintain it. An analog mindset also mirrors how previous generations in under-represented groups generally did work. Middle class Black

Boomers were not generally in a workplace that existed within the context of the digital age. They didn't seek to grab change by the horns before it grabbed them, and they didn't exist in a cultural context that included them within the workplace or without. People of color and other under-represented groups who are stuck in this analog mindset and continue to reinforce the current White, male power structure that centers whatever is White will even undercut other people of color like themselves. This is an outgrowth of White privilege. People of color with the analog mindset and dialed into White privilege will also question why people like them try to lead or strive for more—or attempt to navigate this new work context, which is highly digital, rapidly shifting, ever-changing and demands that leaders not sit idol. Rockstar leadership makes them extremely uncomfortable, and some will work to undo it for those of us who go for it. In every case that I've experienced toxic work environments where I was undermined, maligned or usurped in the workplace, there was always a person of color or another under-represented group member working to poison leadership against me or they were willingly doing the biddings of a toxic White leader. Those members of under-represented groups smile in your face, and do the dirty work when you're not around. Over the course of my career, they have been Asian, LatinX and Black and yes, even White women. It did not matter. As the old folks say, "All skinfolk, ain't kinfolk." And as the Gen Zers say, "Karen will call the manager on you."

The case for culture in leadership

In one of my most popular keynotes, I provide five reasons why Black women should lead in the workplace. I retell the not-so-familiar story of how a Black woman, who some described as a "washed up disco queen," engaged five qualities to officially usher in hip-hop toward the end of disco's reign. She also produced the very first commercial hip-hop single, "Rapper's Delight," much to the chagrin of far more well-known rap acts in New York at the time.

Her name was Sylvia Robinson. She displayed the same characteristics that well-known women leaders in Science Technology Engineering and Math (STEM) have displayed. You probably wouldn't see Ms. Robinson's name aligned with the likes of Mae Jemison, the first Black woman astronaut to go on a space shuttle mission, or Google's Marian Croak who holds the patent to the voting technology that fuels American Idol. You probably wouldn't see Ms. Robinson's name aligned with Jessica O. Matthews, who invented technology that enables soccer balls to illuminate small huts in Africa so that children can do their homework despite the lack of electricity. All the children have to do is kick the ball around during the day to charge it. All of these women are innovative, creative, resilient, transformational and over credentialed. The also operated in the margins, as so many of us do.

Innovation. Black women have a long history of making something out of nothing, the very definition of innovation. But we do so many times due to lack of resources or access. Ms. Robinson had an idea. She wanted to have one of these young rappers who were throwing parties in warehouses in the rough parts of New York "spit" over the beats of the most popular disco tune at that time—"Good Times" by Nile Rogers and Chic. But they'd have to move quickly, and she could. She built a studio in her home.

Resilience. Black women have been told no, over and over again, and still we stand in the face of adversity and deliver, time after time. We eat no for breakfast, no matter what form it comes in. It is said that Ms. Robinson made the rounds to some of the biggest acts to see if they wanted to be the first to record rap, and time and again, she was told no—and by names like Curtis Blow, Grandmaster Flash and others. It's reported that they chuckled at the fact that a woman was trying this, and none of them thought rap should be commercialized. But, Ms. Robinson used these *nos* to to move forward to her groundbreaking yes.

Creativity. Studies show that creativity can spring from lack of resources. Historically, that has been a Black woman's plight; therefore, we can riff with the best of them. Creativity is at the core of innovation. Ms. Robinson, a little bent, but not broken, it's told, walked into a pizza parlor and asked the first person she found behind the counter if he could rap. He said, "Yes, and so can my brother in the back." She had them "spit" on the spot, gathered one more friend and headed to her home studio to record what would become "Rapper's Delight" in one take, the song driven by the very popular baseline of the chart-topping "Good Times."

Transformational leadership. Because we are resilient, we have the courage and willingness to take on tasks that others won't, which has been evident in the "cleanups" of various companies that were in "hot water" of sorts. They hired a Black woman and, my goodness, it got fixed in record time. We are also building our own businesses more than any other segment, according to the U.S. Census. Ms. Robinson literally ushered in the age of hip- hop when disco was fading. She read the tealeaves and jumped on the opportunity for change. She took her new single to a radio station in New York where she had relationships, and they played the song. "Rapper's Delight" became the first commercialized rap song in history. It's safe to say that to this day, just about anyone can rap the lyrics or at least recognize the song.

Credentials. In most cases, Black women are over-credentialed, according to the U.S. Census. Black women hold more advanced degrees than any other group. Ms. Robinson wasn't known for her time in college, if she even went, but she was known for singing behind the likes of Chaka Khan, Ike and Tina and other big names in R&B. She also had her own chart-topping disco singles. She was a well-known songwriter, and with the money she made and the relationships she held, she built that home studio and made history.

Innovative, resilient, creative, transformational and over-credentialed not only describe Sylvia Robinson, these words describe me and so many of my peers, mentors and sponsors. I didn't just wake up one day to realize I possessed these qualities, however. And there are times when I have forgotten.

I have moved boldly in and out of Corporate America over my career, mostly because I did not know any better. My parents told me I could do anything when I was four years old. They showed me Philippians 4:13 in the Bible to prove it, and I believed them. In the early 1940s-1950s, my great-grandmother ran a grocery store about the size of a Publix or Kroger all by herself in Tyler, Texas—with a gun on her hip. We called her Big Mama. So, I guess fear just doesn't exactly flow through my veins like you might expect. Innovation, resilience, transformational leadership, going for plenty of credentials and creativity are in my DNA, and I run to the risk to build or fix things. Sometimes, we simply need the reminder that we are just as entitled as everyone else to every good thing.

You're entitled, so let's flip privilege.

It was January 12, 2020. One of my closest girlfriends in Chicago direct-messaged (DM) me.

"Sis, I need your advice." This wasn't an odd request, and DMing on Instagram had somewhat become our thing. About my girlfriend though: she is no one's slouch. She is one of those Black women that the U.S. Census pointed to, being over credentialed, brilliant, living in a high-rise with her family of four in downtown Chicago and an entrepreneur. Having home-schooled her exceptional kids for years, she still managed to find time to become a published author of several children's books and a graduate of Howard Law.

"I'm trying not to be my old self, you know, the one who would go AWF," she wrote.

She then began to chronicle the story of a bookstore she had dealt with that never formalized paperwork to sell her book. However, she learned on Twitter sometime later that they were indeed selling the book. She was hot, and she had a right to be. She wanted to know what to do. She was leaning toward giving them a piece of her, no, her whole highly-educated mind. Instead, the coach in me asked her, "What would the attorney in you do?" She didn't yet answer. She was still ranting, and the words were scrolling the screen, and fast! Then she came around to a response.

"The attorney weighs the costs and says forget it," she replied.

So I asked, "How can you turn this into an opportunity?"

"You mean I shouldn't go off?" she asked. And I responded with an LOL then said, "What would a White man do in this situation?" Then there was a full stop in the rampant text stream for a good 5 minutes.

"Would he respond in writing and aim to optimize the relationship and opportunity?" I asked.

"So don't go off?" she asked. She really wanted to get these people.

"Just reach deep down, and grab for some privilege.

Perhaps a firmly worded letter that spells out opportunity would not only salvage the relationship, but open doors for more coins," I suggested.

"So I need to just reach for some of the audacity that White men have..." Then she really began to brainstorm great ways to make this opportunity lucrative.

"A White man would show up with a whole end-of-aisle display, asking where should I place this for all of my books." She was catching on. "So I'm right to just behave, right?" she asked.

"White men would see opportunity and not let the anger get the best of the deal," I said. "This is my mantra. I first elevate and ask, 'What would Jesus would do?' Then I get into my flesh and I ask, 'How would a White man approach it?'"

Posing the question is not to center his White maleness, but to gain best practices for getting stuff done. Get as many coins as possible," I added. Lots of crying, giggling emojis came my way.

"I can do this. I'm going to think about this, and put this into action," she said.

And then I gave her the clincher: "The goal is to make the offending party mumble under their breath these words, 'Who does she think she is?!'"

I knew this to be true. The minute I ever carried myself as if I was entitled to the same things as anyone who was privileged or walked with authority, even before I opened my mouth and said something, this was the inevitable reaction from naysayers. I also knew that most privileged White men and women, when walking into a room, a store, a workplace, a park, any space, automatically viewed themselves as being in charge. That's one way to look at privilege.

Shout out to Central Park's Amy Cooper who nearly choked out her dog on its leash before calling the police on Christian Cooper, a Black man who acted like he was in charge and told her to leash the sweet beast. See how it works? It infuriated Amy who forgot all her liberal mindedness and went "all Karen" on the gentleman. I can only imagine how many times she mumbled, "Who does he think he is?!" under her breath before playacting on the phone with police. She isn't the first, and she has male cousins whom I call "Kyle." What's more, people who are not White, often assume that White people are in charge before they ever open their mouths to say a word.

I learned this while pitching new business for my agency back in the early 2000's. I had two White male consultants on my team who were there to work on the business day to day, but they were also there to close our deals sometimes to placate the bigots who didn't believe I was in charge.

They were also handy when it came to confusing the progressives who only for a moment (or more) thought the two White male consultants were the bosses and I wasn't. Either way, my agency was there to get the deal and get their money. I wouldn't let emotions get in the way of that. This is White Businessman 101.

"OMG!" she said. "I'm putting that on my board. That's the goal! To make them say, 'Who does she think she is?!'"

"Exactly, Sis! Put that on your vision board!" Lots of crying giggling emojis flowed through the thread once again, and then she thanked me.

Moving past emotion to opportunity

Lean in and let me ask you, my Sisters who are Black, Latina or Asian or something else: how often do we as women of color get so caught up in the reactionary emotion that we are unable to see the opportunities that are clearly in front of us? I get it. We usually get the short end of the stick. In this case, for my friend, she got the short stick from our own people. That's maddening! It is absolutely something that makes us angry, and we feel all the emotions. The temptation is to act on those emotions, and we all know as educated women, that decisions made with our emotions are never the best ones.

Perhaps White men don't find themselves in these situations as often as we do. I'm not certain, but I've noticed that White men and even White women in business have no problem continuing to pursue business with entities that they may not even like.

It's definitely cultural. As Black women our first inclination is to cut the entity off, block them, tune them out. It is likely to protect ourselves as a fight or flight tendency. Our people have been through so much historically. Because we have, we have learned to accept less from ourselves and from others who are like us. This is the otherness syndrome that privilege promotes. It takes others to surround and center the privileged party, assign value to them, and reinforce and devalue the "others."

Otherness is essential to privilege. It wouldn't exist without it. Think about it: why would anyone decide to sell books without something in writing or without some other way to pay the author for their stock? I'm sure their intentions were not devious, but something in their minds gave them permission to do so. When we don't assign value to an item or thing, we likely will toss it aside or not handle it with care. The same is true with people and relationships. If we do not assign value to a person or a relationship, chances are we will not treat them with the same care as someone on whom we place high value. Do you believe that if Barack Obama's people provided books to the shop, that the owners would attempt to sell the book without express permission in writing? The answer is probably not, because the shop owner would have assigned value to the former President. They would have also known that doing something like that could have far- reaching repercussions. The former President still occupies the expansive privilege having once resided in the White House. Ironically, however, we saw in some instances while he was in office where even that privilege did not pre-empt the otherness that being Black in America can provoke. There were still White people who believed they could police him, that they were still the boss of him, his tan suit, Michelle's bare arms, the children's social lives, only for starters.

It is still a bit dumbfounding that my dear friend, the Howard Law alumna and well-known blogger (she was on *The Oprah Show* once) didn't command some value with those bookstore owners, simply by being an author with a popular children's book; yet, sometimes, other people of color can "other" you as a result of their very own "otherness."

As well, our people are more communal by origin. We share. We're in it together. We'll look out for each other. You're my sister. You're my brother. We are family. Contracts came along with capitalism, not community. That is our default. Not, "I'm in charge of you, and I'm here to tell you what to do." But we have to learn how to leverage that very sentiment in a society that is essentially fueled by it, especially the hierarchy of Corporate America.

It's all about eagles and chickens.

I can't repeat enough, however, that owning your entitlement as a daughter of God can throw people. I wish that I could assure you that when you decide to make a pact with yourself to assign yourself value, to know yourself, that you will instantly inspire everyone, that everyone will celebrate your new-found position as an eagle. Unfortunately, owning the fact that you are entitled will nearly guarantee that there are people who will instantly not like you for doing so. But as a few of my wise mentors have told me occasion, eagles do not bother themselves with the business of chickens. If they do, they are flying too low. In order to soar like an eagle, you have to accept that everyone isn't an eagle and be ok with it. Chickens will not center an eagle, in fact, clucking and staying low to the ground is their only mission besides laying an occasional egg, which makes for someone's breakfast or at best, another chicken.

There is one exception: beware of chickens disguised as eagles. There are small-minded people in very high places. They have self-serving motivations. They don't understand you. Some won't like you, simply because you soar with excellence and may not have the title to go along with it yet. They will fool you. They smile at you, even have small talk in the elevator. As you are busy not minding the chickens in the coop, beware that every once in a while, a chicken in an eagle's outfit may make themselves known. Some chickens have considerably more clout, rank and influence, but didn't attain these with the excellence and rockstar qualities you exude. They despise your shine. They don't know how you know the things you do, and it threatens them.

Chickens will try everything to destroy you. How do you combat them? You can fend them off with other true eagles in your tribe with as much power or more. This means that you will need more than one or two eagles whom you can text message or call unannounced.

As I assured my friend, one way to know that you are on track is to listen for the clucking of the chickens, even from those fake eagles. If you get rumblings of the statement, "Who does she think she is?" you are likely on the right track.

Coaching question: When you enter a space, what are you doing to impact the way others see you? If it is positive, how can you find the opportunity in it? If it is negative, how can you counter it?

***

9 WAIT ONE MINUTE BEFORE YOU ACCEPT THAT DIVERSITY & INCLUSION ROLE, SIS...

We need more Black women in the C-Suite, yes. I'd like to qualify that statement, however. We need more Black women in CXO roles, not simply Chief Diversity Officers (CDO). I've held this notion for quite some time, and we're finally beginning to see business media and other experts taking on the topic. This role does not have profit and loss (P&L) responsibility, which is a requirement on your resume before you can begin to think about securing the most prominent CXO roles, especially CEO. According to a recent study called "The Black P&L Leader" by the Executive Leadership Council (ELC), commissioned by Korn Ferry and sponsored by The UPS Foundation, there are only four Black CEOs in the Fortune 500. As we know, none of them are women. It found that most of the Black leaders they identified were not only capable of taking on P&L roles, but despite their competency, they continue to be relegated to leadership roles in HR, corporate social responsibility and yes, D&I. It has yet to be proven that any of the people who take these D&I roles are included in a succession plan. Only a precious few in the Fortune 500 have direct reporting status to the CEO. Chief Diversity Officers have such broad responsibilities for every under-represented group known to man. As a result, the all-encompassing nature of the D&I programs are watered down when attempting to attack systemic issues like racism and sexism head-on. Intersectionality is rarely addressed. If you happen to be a Black CDO, you can't be 'too Black" or look out for Black interests too much. You're typically strapped for budget. You are expected to be all things to all people. White men even knock on your door requesting acknowledgment for their own employee resource group, and your role is to hear them out. I've even seen White women attempt to take leadership roles in employee resource groups of color, and the job of the CDO is to give this non-sense an audience. The role is more diplomat than change agent.

My problem isn't simply with this role. It's with diversity and inclusion roles at every level in every business unit. Whether they are in marketing, technology, human resources and corporate social responsibility or beyond, Black women tend to take these roles more than anyone else. The reasons are simple: we have a passion for what we perceive to be "the work" of equality. It's something we yearn for personally, and we've likely been somewhat vocal about the topic within the company. This can be a slippery slope. I've had clients tell me horror stories about being "tapped" for the diversity, equity and inclusion "committee" with no discussion of an expanded position description, compensation or title change. They are as junior as second-level managers who are now faced with having daily conversations with the CEO, CPO and other executives. They are being asked to do expert work, but not being compensated for it or provided with the proper resources.

Many Black women fail to ask the right questions before taking one of these assignments from the C-Suite on down to "committee head." We seem to be super excited to take the roles because we feel that finally, we've been seen, and we are now having conversations at the executive level about issues that really mean something to us personally. We think we have a chance at impacting the greater good. You're finally getting pulled into meetings with the real decision makers.

Dream job, right? Not so fast, Sis. There are very real questions you should ask before taking a role like this, even if it has a C in the title. First, I'd like to raise a question: how many CDOs have you seen ascend to another C-Suite role within the same company? Do they ever even become the Chief People Officer? A Wall Street Journal article in July 2020 finally exposed what we knew: "It's one of the hottest job in America—and it has a revolving door." These jobs have incredible turnover, and they generally don't seem to solve the diversity and inclusion problem in companies. There are a precious few model companies at the top of the *DiversityInc* Top 50 list each year. Dig into the numbers, and you will find the very same gushing hole in their leadership pipeline for Black women, if we are even represented in the numbers at all. Corporate leaders need to stop and think before they tap that person of color simply because they are a person of color and have shown passion around the topic of anti-racism... just stop. This is also unfair to Black employees. It happens to us more than to anyone else and especially right now. I've seen this happen, and when things don't go the way White leaders think they should, they push the Black employees aside and hire a D&I consultant or firm from the outside. In some cases, they may even hire someone from outside of the company and give them a real title, perks and C-Suite adjacency, or better. Many aren't offered anything but the role of "committee head." They offer no budget, but entice them with C-Suite conversations.

My Sisters, when they come to you with this request, ask these questions for starters:

1. Will you increase my pay?
2. Will you provide resources like headcount and consultants?
3. Is there budget?
4. How will my title change?
5. What is my career path?
6. What does success in this role look like, and how will it be measured?
7. What are expectations around true, systemic change when it comes to race?

And if you are offered a CDO role, please ask where you are in the succession plan. If you do not receive solid answers that support your goals, just say, "No!" The bottom line is this: don't stunt for these companies unless they are willing to stunt for you.

My D&I story

Once upon a time, I took one of these roles. The year was 2013. I was minding my own business, rocking my 3-month-old to sleep after her midday bottle when my smartphone lit up. It was my first supervisor, a partner at a massive agency. He was embedded at a company that used to be a client, and that I had incredible respect for. Ultimately, he asked me to come work for that company. I wasn't in the market for a position. I'd worked for two decades, about half that time running a small agency that had represented some pretty recognizable brands. I'd just left a global agency as a Senior Vice President. I wanted this time to be a mother to my new little one, so I'd decided that consulting here and there was the most that I would do, if anything. But this call came from a person whom I cherished, and he was working for two more people that I cherished and respected, including the SVP of corporate communications who had been my client twice over at two different agencies. All three of them are White, but that didn't matter one bit. Yet, I took a real pause. They were asking me to do something that at least twice in my career I had turned down. I had vowed to myself never to take a diversity & inclusion or multicultural marketing role ever in my career. Full stop.

This story may surprise you, because many of you know me as "that woman with the strawberry blonde curly afro that used to rock the stage for the number one advertiser in the world about diversity & inclusion." You're right. About eight times between 2017 and 2018, Brand Innovators' Co-Founder Marc Sternberg passed me the mic in various cities, at the headquarters of major brands and agencies to share what would become my signature message concerning inclusion marketing.

The obvious plot twist is that I took the position, but why did I do it if I was so vehemently opposed to roles like it? You may have even noted that I took a lesser position than I'd had in the past. I made VP before I was 30, and here I was more than a decade later doing something I said I'd never do. Let's start with why I made that vow to begin with. I remember telling the executive partner at the global agency where I cut my teeth, far less eloquently than I'd deliver my keynotes nearly 20 years later:

"I want to do strategic communications for White people too. "

I never will forget the look on this leader's face when I said that. I warned you that it wasn't eloquent. I went on to say that they had hired me to do technology PR, and I didn't want anyone to forget that I had talents in strategic communications that reached far beyond diversity & inclusion because 1) it's always the program with the least budget and first to get cut. 2) I didn't want to be pigeonholed—not this early in my career.

Within moments, she composed herself, smiled and said, "I totally get it." She'd asked me to take over an entire practice after only two years at the agency. Most would have jumped at the opportunity, and it was a compliment to my abilities. I told her that I would support, but I didn't want to stop doing the other important work I was doing for Fortune 500 brands on their roster.

So, back to 2013...what shifted? Beyond the fact that the three people inside this Fortune 10 were some of the same people from that agency where I put my stake in the ground against a multicultural role, something in the cultural context was about to shift. You see, when I ran my own agency, I did work for some major beauty brands. One in particular was looking at how to address a trend that the 2000 Census uncovered: America was browning. The most-checked box that year was the "other" box, despite what was publicized. We'd been told that the Hispanic population was the fastest-growing community. That wasn't incorrect. It was just a box that was recognized as a "race." The "other" box was not. So for years since then, the "other" box would still be checked most, but everyone seemed to ignore it. This beauty company was literally developing products based on the changing curl patterns in people's hair. Stylists were reporting fewer blondes in their chairs for service and more people looking to straighten or tame their curls. That insight stuck with me, and I also knew that by 2017 we would begin to see predictions that people of color would become the majority. Suddenly, there was a real business case for me to dive into the multicultural space, because in only a few years, the so-called "general market" team would need counsel from someone like me. Additionally, after 20 years of building a solid reputation in the industry, it would be pretty hard to be pigeonholed. To do this work for a company that I believed really walked the talk was also a golden opportunity. After all, I'd have to believe that in order to put my name or face on the work. It would be the perfect time to take on one of these roles and bring my classic marketing approach and award-winning skills to an area that didn't always get the premium talent, but mostly the most passionate talent. Budget limitations dictate everything, even talent decisions. I did, however proclaim from the start that it would be my first and last diversity gig.

You still may be puzzled at why I'd make that statement. I worked at this Fortune 10, did more than what I signed up to do, and I created some great waves in the industry. My team won award after award, and now, here I am. Despite the wonderful, standout work and commitment of companies like that one, have you noticed that we, here in the U.S., really are still in the very same place? In fact, some would say we've regressed. I liken D&I and multicultural positions to organic fruit. You've all purchased those beautiful bright red strawberries. They are delicious, but we all know what happens if you don't cook with them or eat them quickly. They rot. They mold and they're no good to anyone. You can quickly tire in these roles because they aren't just jobs. Many times, you find yourself in hand-to-hand, mortal combat because leaders and colleagues are stuck in the old way—that D&I and multicultural efforts really belong over there—in that corner, not taking up space in their world where the "real work is done." I'm older and wiser now, and my perspective is clearer with a bit of hindsight on my side.

Did you know that 30 years after John Johnson, founder and publisher of *Ebony Magazine*, launched the first diversity marketing campaign with a major advertiser, no one single company has solved for diversity & inclusion? Yes, more companies tout it as a value. Yes, more brands are making statements and standing in solidarity with under-represented groups. But how many are actually sustaining a commitment to supplier diversity, creating viable leadership pipelines for diverse talent across the business and building diversity & inclusion into their technology business and operations on an ongoing basis? Are they creating measurable key performance indicators (KPIs) with the goal to ultimately eradicate the problem? One reason companies may not have cracked the code is that the problem isn't clearly defined. Many are so busy trying to lump every issue into one effort or one watered down statement or one program that it completely misses the mark. We have brands that are afraid to say the word Black, let alone the word racism. And yet, there are other key issues that brands overlook when attempting to market and be on the right side of history.

My Sister, you can indeed take a role like this. I'm simply saying, go in with your eyes open, and put your brand first. My story underscores the reasons why:

You need to have solid, one-to-one relationships with your White leaders to pull this off with some success. You'll need to have a desire to work for the company to begin with, however.

Check out the company's reputation for with dealing with Black senior leaders and those in the ranks. This should drive some of your decision-making. It is a reflection of how they view you.

Know that it takes the entire company, from the C-Suite down, to commit sustaining budget to these programs to really move the needle. Will you have that?

Assess whether you will be able to craft an authentic and empathetic positioning the in the market year over year. When it is time to hold up a statement that says the company stands in solidarity with Black people, you can be certain that your Black employees aren't unhappy or non-existent. Remember that this is your reputation too.

Are your marketing leaders advocating for Black talent on the various marketing teams in a safe environment where their voices can be heard? If your role is in marketing itself, you need to know if this is the environment you really want to sign up for. Are Black team members' ideas hijacked? Marketing is the "face" of the company, and if the marketing doesn't reflect inclusion, your work will be cut out for you.

Is this company willing to challenge racism in your workplace head-on? I've seen time and again racism written off as politics, unconscious bias or a personality conflict, and White privilege takes precedence over what's right.

Is the company willing to bring D&I out of the shadows to the business as usual environment, valuing your counsel in all of the business? White privilege can take over in these cases, centering their decision making and thinking over your counsel.

I spend much of my time coaching leaders who fear taking these D&I or multicultural roles in any part of the business because of the implications for their careers. Others are leaders who are experiencing microaggressions, and their careers have been stalled. They feel they've hit the Black ceiling. All of them realize that the path to the C- Suite only allows a precious few to pass through. I also spend time with leaders at corporations who want to make an impact for their team members, especially the Black and Brown ones.

So yes, consider these roles, but buyer beware.

Coaching question: How will you shift the way you approach D&I roles when it comes to your leadership goals?

***

10. ONE LAST THING

My Sister, we will definitely have more conversations like these. This is only the beginning. With the world, and our country in particular, in such turmoil, I encourage you to seek out the opportunities for you in it. Rockstar leadership doesn't just happen. You need to be intentional about it, and I'm here to support you. In books to come, we will delve deeper into the concept of flipping privilege to your advantage, building and activating your tribe, leaning out to lean in, building a recession-proof personal brand, becoming that transformational leader with an entrepreneurial mindset and wielding weapons of mass innovation. We'll even delve into some small business topics for those who want to transition or start one. I'm so happy to share this time with you, and that you've allowed me into your space. Keep striving.

To corporate leaders who are also reading, it's your time to stand for what is best for your business and best for women of color and Black women especially. I usually begin my messages with storytelling, and while I could tell any number of stories of my experiences with discrimination in Corporate America, I want to humanize this message by focusing the discussion on you—the leader who actually has some decision-making power to do something about the Black employee experience in your workplace.

I'll start by asking this question: How will you move this important conversation about racism forward in the workplace so that it benefits employees? First, we need not be afraid of the word. Say it. *Racism.* It's as if it's been struck from the corporate lexicon. It's an unwritten rule not to use that word unless the EEOC is involved. By then, it's too late. We need to move beyond that. Yes, most people now get that Black colleagues are traumatized by events like the murder of George Floyd, but have you considered how events like this are literally and inextricably linked to the experience in the workplace for your Black employees? It is indeed tethered. Consider that racism in the U.S. has been a smoldering crisis for nearly 400 years—that not only do your Black colleagues bring that trauma in with them every day, systemic racism also comes to work with their colleagues on every level. Yes, there are racists in your halls. It's shocking to consider. We've found nice words for it, and it typically is a lot cleaner and more professional looking than that video of the police officer with his knee dug into George Floyd's neck. It even has better, more palatable names: bias, unconscious or not. But the effect and the root of it is all the same. Career and character assassinations that happen daily do immediate and long-term damage to people's very livelihoods. Sidelined, stifled, even strangled talents that are no doubt incredible contributors and credentialed, hit the Black ceiling in Corporate America because of microaggressions and discrimination. And no, they won't call HR because or fear of reprisal or being deemed a troublemaker. They may not even want to take the time out of their lives or their peace to even consider how these investigations and legal actions can drain their souls and pocketbooks, let alone their reputations. So most people just take it, and then return to work the next day. After all, it's how our parents did it.

The stories my father has told me about being a first generation computer programmer and being demeaned on a daily basis make my heartbreak, but I reasoned in my mind that that was the 60s. And while much of what he experienced was more overt, the covert discrimination still lives on in 2020. It's time we call it out. To add insult to injury, there is an extremely broken-to-nearly-non-existent pipeline for Black women to leadership. A precious few make it to the top, not many.

Four years after her retirement, we are still waiting for the next Ursula Burns, retired CEO of Xerox and the first and only Black woman to sit at the helm of a Fortune 500. Yet the U.S. Census says that Black women hold more advanced degrees than any other group. Where is the disconnect? How do we begin to take action to change the experience Black employees have in these organizations where White maleness is centered? Think of how many more "teeth" these public statements of solidarity would have if your employees actually could attest to a wonderful employee experience without question or overlooking what happened in that meeting just last week when someone took credit for their idea. What if they actually didn't leave the organization before making it to the executive levels because they were unhappy? What if they trusted you enough to actually let you know what happened? What if they weren't pushed out because of petty, discriminatory leadership that is allowed to stay although everyone knows that leadership is toxic? Employees...all of them... are your most important brand ambassadors, and they carry the story of their experience in your company with them for the rest of their lives. Know that hosting a few town hall meetings or sending out a few employee surveys is not enough. Dedicate dollars that are substantial and sustaining. Make it a priority. It isn't just a job for your D&I business unit to correct what is wrong. This is everyone's responsibility, from the very top, down.

Coaching questions: How will you move from statements to action and incentivize your leadership teams and employees to get involved? How can you ensure that all lives matter by taking a closer look at the quality of Black lives in your organization? Your employees are the community, and they bring the outside into your companies each and everyday. How will you begin to change hearts and minds so that you can really impact change? Big painful moments can bring about big change. I for one can't wait to see what's on the other side. Are you in?

✳✳✳

THE ROCKSTAR LEADERSHIP COACHING GUIDE

THE 7 AFFIRMATIONS

"I know who I am, and I find my value in my story."

"I'll be excellent...and good with the skin I'm in."

"I recognize there indeed is a problem,
and I will confront it."

"I will be my best advocate."

"Some sisters have made it to the C-Suite being
themselves. I can too."

"I will bet on my brand."

"I will take positive cues from white privilege because
I am entitled."

POWERFUL QUESTIONS TO HELP
YOU REACH YOUR GOALS

What are your three superpowers? What are your
three passions?

_____

_____

_____

_____

_____

_____

_____

_____

_____

_____

_____

_____

_____

_____

Now, try your hand at a value proposition. What is
your "one thing"?

_____

_____

How might you shift the way you are showing up to work in order to leverage authenticity as a leader? List 2 small, daily engagements and 2 big gestures.

_____

_____

_____

_____

_____

_____

_____

_____

_____

_____

_____

_____

_____

_____

_____

_____

_____

_____

_____

The next time you are faced with a microaggression, bias or rejection, how will you respond?

_____

_____

_____

_____

_____

_____

_____

_____

_____

_____

_____

_____

_____

_____

_____

_____

_____

_____

_____

_____

_____

What one new step are you willing to take to begin to actively advocate for yourself?

_____

_____

_____

_____

_____

_____

_____

_____

What will you commit to in order to begin to intentionally form and activate your tribe?

_____

_____

_____

_____

_____

_____

_____

How will you leverage your tribe to navigate the corporate politics and bias?

_____

_____

_____

_____

What scares you the most about being all you in the workplace?

_____

_____

_____

_____

_____

_____

_____

What can you do about how you show up that can help overcome that fear?

_____

_____

_____

_____

_____

_____

_____

_____

_____

_____

_____

What one step are you willing to make to begin to build your personal brand to support your leadership goals?

_____

_____

_____

_____

_____

_____

_____

_____

What will you do to communicate your "one thing" in a powerful and meaningful way? How will you engage your CQ to innovate?

_____

_____

_____

_____

_____

_____

_____

_____

_____

_____

_____

When you enter a space, what are you doing to impact the way others see you?

_____

_____

_____

_____

_____

_____

_____

_____

If it is positive, how can you find the opportunity in it? If it is negative, how can you counter it?

_____

_____

_____

_____

_____

_____

_____

_____

_____

_____

_____

_____

_____

_____

_____

How will you shift the way you approach D&I roles when it comes to your leadership goals?

_____

_____

_____

_____

_____

_____

_____

_____

_____

_____

_____

_____

_____

_____

_____

_____

_____

_____

_____

_____

_____

COACHING QUESTIONS FOR CORPORATE
DECISION MAKERS

How will you move from statements to action and
incentivize your leadership teams and employees to
get involved?

_____

_____

_____

_____

_____

_____

_____

_____

_____

_____

How can you ensure that all lives matter by taking a
closer look at the quality of black lives in your
organization?

_____

_____

_____

_____

_____

_____

_____

_____

Your employees are the community, and they bring the outside into your companies each and everyday. How will you begin to change hearts and minds so that you can really impact change?

_____

_____

_____

_____

_____

_____

_____

_____

_____

_____

_____

_____

_____

_____

_____

_____

_____

_____

_____

ACKNOWLEDGMENTS

I come from the tradition of the Black Baptist Church, so it wouldn't be right not to begin by giving honor to God, but I also want to acknowledge my parents: James and Media Smith who were betting on my brand long before I even knew I had one. I'd also like to acknowledge my sister, Dr. C. Joyce Price for always setting the bar high as we moved through life, but always being my best friend. I'd be remiss if I didn't mention Michael Lehman of Lehman & Lehman Company and his main client Joseph "Rev Run" Simmons who urged Michael to help me get my "untethered" journey underway. It was Rev and his son Diggy's manager Uncle Perry who lovingly fussed at me a little backstage at the Essence Festival to take my Instagram profile off private mode because "people needed to know who you are."

Michael helped me score that first meeting with one of the major publishing houses in New York City. I never will forget the Uber ride over to the publisher, arranged by Michael. I was on the line with Valorie Burton, now my mentor coach, but my longtime girlfriend for many, many years. I was determined to get her to tell me what to say in the meeting, and she was determined to get the story on how I was actually walking into a Big 5 publisher with absolutely nothing in hand but a pitch in my head. She told me then that I was well on my way to being a well-known author because of how rare it is to be invited into the halls of a Big 5 publisher. I would return two more times, and I shall return to meetings like that again.

Thank you to my book coach, Toure, who said to me so accurately "Together, we rise." His insights and connections have been key to this journey.

To Jaylen Bledsoe, of Bledsoe Collective, who's also been the angel on my right shoulder throughout this process, hyping me up when needed, recommending me and sharing publishing contacts and advice when needed.

To all my clients who have made this journey possible and all of their rich stories and experiences that undergird my content, I thank you as well.

Shout-out to my dear sisterfriend Eva Greene Wilson, aka SocaMom®, who is always a text or DM away to share everything from business, virtual event planning, publishing, podcasting and even man talk. I appreciate your allowing me to allow others into our conversations to make a point about privilege.

I would be remiss not to thank Ashley Blaker, my dear friend, confidant, former boss and former agency lead and nearly family. Ashley was there when all of these opportunities began presenting themselves, when all of the ideas became concepts. When book proposals manifested, when job opportunities presented themselves. He is the best listener and always has wise counsel. Talk about an awesome tribe member!

Thanks to my pastor Rev. Bryan L. Carter and First Lady Stephanie Carter of Concord Church in Dallas. Thank you for always swooping in with a shout-out, encouragement or a bouquet of congratulations.

Finally, a hearty thanks to Gaye Arbuckle, Minister of Music at Concord, who over the years has just randomly called, texted or pulled me over to the side to let me know that I am doing "God's work" in supporting people on their journeys to having better lives and being better leaders. She always tells me, "Don't stop!!"

Guess what?

I won't.

***

ABOUT THE AUTHOR

L. Michelle Smith is the CEO/founder of no silos communications llc, the parent company for six media, content, talent development and strategic communications consulting brands, all fueled by tech. She has more than 25 years of experience as an elite, award-winning strategic communicator at global agencies, her own boutique agency and a Fortune 10 technology, telecom and media company. She develops rockstar leaders and brands that thrive at the intersection of tech, business and culture. She is a certified executive and business coach. She is also the creator, executive producer and host of The Culture Soup Podcast® which is enjoyed in 38 countries and on every continent. Previously, she raced to the officer ranks in no time in her career, making vice president before the age of 30. Then she "fell" into entrepreneurship, marking their million-dollar milestone in year 5. She's held officer-level positions for about half her career. She is one of the most sought-after, contemporary keynote speakers, facilitators, panelists and hosts on topics surrounding technology, business and culture. She has been featured across the country on some of the most important stages across multiple industries. L. Michelle has been an official contributor to *Black Enterprise*, and she is an adjunct professor of strategic communications at the Bob Schieffer College of Communications at Texas Christian University where she also sits on the Board of Visitors.

www.ingramcontent.com/pod-product-compliance
Lightning Source LLC
Chambersburg PA
CBHW060645150426
42811CB00085B/2419/J